Waynesburg Co
Waynesburg, F

335.977234   I39n
Indiana Historical Commission
New Harmony as seen by participants and travelers
110471

The American Utopian Adventure

SERIES TWO

NEW HARMONY AS SEEN BY PARTICIPANTS
AND TRAVELERS

Plan de New-Harmony, par C. A. Lesueur

NEW HARMONY
AS SEEN BY PARTICIPANTS AND TRAVELERS

PART ONE
Letters of William Pelham, written in 1825 and 1826
PART TWO
Account of a visit to New Harmony, by Karl Bernhard, Duke of Saxe-Weimar-Eisenach
PART THREE
Diary and recollections of Victor Colin Duclos

WITH CONTEMPORARY ILLUSTRATIONS BY
CHARLES ALEXANDRE LESUEUR

PORCUPINE PRESS

Philadelphia 1975

These selections were first published in *Indiana as Seen by Early Travelers,* selected and edited by Harlow Lindley (Indianapolis: Indiana Historical Commission, 1916)

Reprinted with new illustrations 1975 by
PORCUPINE PRESS, INC.
Philadelphia, Pennsylvania 19107

Library of Congress Cataloging in Publication Data
Indiana. Historical Commission.
  New Harmony as seen by participants and travelers.

  (The American utopian adventure, ser. 2)
  Selections reprinted from Indiana as seen by early travelers.
  CONTENTS: Letters of William Pelham, written in 1825 and 1826.--Bernhard, K. Account of a visit to New Harmony.--Diary and recollections of Victor Colin Duclos.
  1. New Harmony, Ind.--History. 2. Harmony Society. I. Title.
HX656.N5I52   1975   335'.9'77234   74-32002
ISBN 0-87991-028-3

Manufactured in the United States of America

PART ONE

From *Letters of William Pelham, written in 1825 and 1826.*

These letters were written by William Pelham to his son, William Creese Pelham of Zanesville, Ohio, in 1825 and 1826. The original letters are in the possession of the children of the late Louis Pelham at New Harmony, Indiana. The letters describe William Pelham's journey down the Ohio, stopping at Maysville, Cincinnati, Louisville and Mt. Vernon, with the arrival at New Harmony, where " a new society was about to be formed." They tell of the appearance of the town and mention some of the people gathering there, express unbounded enthusiasm for Robert Owen and his plans for improving the condition of society and describes many of the pleasures and hardships and daily life experienced during some months of the preliminary Society.

William Pelham was born in Williamsburg, Virginia, in 1759, a younger son of Peter Pelham and Ann Creese of Boston, and grand-son of Peter Pelham, of the Pelhams of Chichester, Sussex, England, who was the first mezzotint engraver in America. The family of this elder Pelham is described in the life of John Singleton Copley, the artist, whose mother married Mr. Pelham, as a household of unusual culture and congeniality, and the only one in New England at that time where painting and engraving were the predominant pursuits.

William Pelham when just grown to manhood, was for three years a surgeon in the American Revolution, the older brother whom he met at Maysville being Maj. Gen. Charles Pelham of Virginia. From his journals and account books, he seems to have taken passage more than once for England and at one time to have spent several years there. In a letter written in French, dated London, 1793, he says that the climate of London would break down the constitution of a man of iron and that he will return to his native land as it does not take an iron constitution to live in the climate of Virginia.

He evidently left England determined to change his profession as well as climate for about the year 1800 he opened a book shop and publishing house in Boston, selling out in 1811 and removing to Newark, New Jersey, and the following year to Philadelphia. At this time his young son, William Creese Pelham, was a pupil in the Neef school at the Falls of the Schuylkill and from this time a close friendship with the Neef family continued through their lives.

Having secured some land in Ohio through the Virginia Grant of 1812, William Pelham brought his family west in 1816 and began editing the Ohio Republic at Zanesville. In 1818 he was appointed postmaster and these pursuits he continued until he resigned to come to New Harmony in 1825.

Mr. Pelham was a scholarly man, a deep thinker, delicate in mind and constitution, and his long life as a servant of the public had wearied him of the grasping ways of the world and Robert Owen's communistic plans seemed to him a Utopia of peace for his declining years. So after much reading and some correspondence[1] relative to the matter, he came to New

---

1. A letter from William Owen, son of Robert Owen, will be found following the Pelham letters.

Harmony as described in these letters. From the letters we learn he found occupation at once in the accounting department of the store and when the Gazette was published he became one of the first editors. His son joined him in the spring of 1826 and the following year William Pelham purchased a farm near Mt. Vernon and died very suddenly at his home there on February third, 1827. He passed away just two months before the final dissolution of the society which had filled his last years with a great enthusiasm and interest.

CAROLINE CREESE PELHAM.

Opposite Buffington's Island,
Ohio River, Monday,
1st Aug., 1825,
3 o'clock, P. M.

My Dear Son:—

I have concluded to commence a letter at this place which, you will probably receive from Cincinnatti. It would give you pleasure to see how commodiously I am situated on board this boat. She is 70 or 75 feet long abt. 9 feet wide, very deeply laden with flour and destined to Florence in Alabama—navigated by six men beside the Capt., Absalom Boyd, who is a mild, quiet character,— in fact I have experienced nothing but civility and kindness from all on board. The following rude sketch will give you some idea of my local position in the vessel, premising that at Point Harmar I had a box or bunk made 6f. by $4\frac{1}{2}$ to contain the whole of my bed & bedding. . . . . [Sketch omitted.]

The right side is boarded up, & the whole covered with a substantial roof except the bow & stern. On the roof stands the caboose & the rowers here exercise themselves with 2 and sometimes 4 sweeps which they ply pretty constantly. At the foot of my bunk is an opening in the side of the vessel about 4 by 5 feet, closed at night by 2 folding shutters.

I am now sitting on the foot of my bed, my feet resting on a footboard placed for my convenience by one of my ship-mates. As my bunk is placed on 2 tier of barrels there is abundant space between my head & the roof of the boat. Capt. Boyd and myself lodge together, my bed being sufficiently large for both.

In the article of diet I do not fare so well, as I cannot relish the provision cooked for the crew; & have therefore lived almost entirely on tea & coffee & cheese. Give my kind compliments to Mrs. Mills and tell her that her friendly piece of cake formed almost the whole of my support from Zanesville to Marietta.

I wrote you a few lines from Marietta, which you will not

receive till Saturday next, (Aug. 6). On carrying it to the P. O. I met with Arius Nye, who informed me that Mr. Morris (whom I have not seen)—is no longer P. M. The fact is, he has been *Hamproned* out of the office by Squire Buell who contrived to convince the P. M. G. [Postmaster General] that he was a fitter person to succeeed Willcox than Morris.—This is the individual system in perfection.

This (Buffington's)—Island is always a troublesome place when the water is low. At some future time I will give you a minute account of the hardship, the labor & fatigue—& the immense, extravagant waste of human strength in navigating this river, &c &c. We have a strong active crew, and they make abundant use of the terms, God—Jesus Christ—Hell-fire & Damnation &c &c. &c., but in a manner somewhat different from the reverend clergy and certainly not with so much worldy profit. The most embarrassing place will be Letart's falls. If anything extraordinary occurs there I will note it, I am greatly at a loss for my Ohio Pilot which unfortunately I left behind, and there is nothing of the sort on board this vessel. I have only Melish's small map of Ohio & Indiana.

I feel greatly indebted to Joel Frazey for his kindness; he left me at N. Ayers Salt works—after a delightful ride. Remember me kindly to him.

Saturday Aug. 5, 11 o'clock A. M. We have just passed Portsmouth & Alexandria at the mouth of the Scioto— the former a neat, and even handsome little town— the latter consisting of 4 or 5 log-houses. We are still abt. 50 miles fr. Maysville, which we shall probably not reach till Monday, for we do not move faster than about 28 or 30 miles a day, & lie by every night. I am told, however, that we shall now get forward much faster than we have done while embarrassed with frequent bars, shoals & ripples. The Capt. & others on board calculate that we shall arrive at Mt. Vernon about the 17th or 18th of this month. By that time, I foresee, that I shall require 5 or 6 days rest on land, in some *quiet* lodging house during which I can refit, & get my clothes and blankets washed. I shall write to you immediately on reaching Mt. Vernon. In the meantime give my most affectionate love to Mary and tell her that her ample provision of tea, coffee, and sugar, will probably last me to the point of my destination.— Present me also my most kindly & affectionately to Mr. Peters. I have seen no newspaper *from any place* since I left Z. [Zanesville] and you would be surprised if you could really estimate the indifference I feel about general or local politics and the contentions of opposite parties. I feel once more free from all this turmoil & shall never engage in it again, whether I return or not. Present my kind respects to Mr. John Peters and Michael—to Mr. Sheward & wife & in general to all friends who may think me worthy of their enquiries.

After leaving Maysville I shall make some additions to this letter and then put into the P. O. at Cincinnati.—Our old friend Jim Marshall (who is one of the hired hands) has just brought me half of a fine, tho small water-melon. I have received much kindness from him.

The *steam* boat Lawrence, worked by *4 horses without steam*, (moving in a circle on her deck) has just passed us on her way up the river.

Direct the Ohio Repub. to W. Pelham, New Harmony, Ind.—on the paper itself—put it in a wrapper in the usual manner & direct the cover to Postmaster New Harmony, Ind. Do not forget to remember me kindly to Messrs. Keightley & Harris & Joel Frezey—& Mr. Mills &c. &c.

Monday 8th Aug. Yesterday afternoon, I had the inexpressable happiness of an affecting and joyful meeting with my brother and sister, after a separation of 39 years and 1 month. At first sight, he did not know me, but immediately recollected me on a nearer approach and for my part, I think I should have recognized him if I had met him in Zanesville—tho' we are both much altered by time. He has an interesting family—his 4 daughters and 2 sons were introduced to me. Chas. & Wm. are gone to Arkansas. Peter & Atkinson also absent—, the former at his station in Florida—the latter in Philad. My stay was necessarily short—& in the evening we passed by Maysville— but the evening was too far advanced for me to gain a distinct view of it. We are now, 11.30 A. M. 22 miles distant from Maysville. My brother's daus. accompanied me to the boat which lay ½ mile from the house. During this walk, the two eldest enquired particularly about you & Mary & expressed an earnest desire to see you both—not unmixed with the hope that you at least wd. make a run in the stage one of these days as far as Maysville.

The weather has been remarkably cool and pleasant on the river, since I left Zanesville—I have not been at all incommoded by heat—I make it a rule not to go on deck in the morning till the sun has dissipated the fog, when there is any—and always to retire to my birth soon after sunset.

We expect to arrive at Cincinn tonight or tomorrow morning. I shall therefore, here close my letter and seal it.

    Yr truly affectionate Father,

          Wm. Pelham.

      On bd Post Boy, Ohio River.
      Wednesd, noon, Aug. 10, 1825.
      32 miles below Cincinn.

My dear Son—

  We reached Cincinnati yesterday abt. 10 A.M. & left it about 6 in the evg. It has been so often and so well described, that it is needless for me to make any remarks on it. In fact I saw but little of the city my attention being almost wholly directed to other objects. What I did see, however, greatly surpassed my expectations. In approaching the city we counted 10 new steam boats on the stocks—besides some under repair. Boats continually passing up and down. It is really a handsome and even elegant town, containing an immense amt. of property.

  As soon as we got to the shore I landed, and walking up the Main street I unexpectedly met our old friend Mr. John Scott, who resides there with his family. After the usual salutations, I enquired for, and he directed me to a first rate barber, who shaved me admirably, and cut off my pigtail!—the inconvenience of which I could no longer endure. While these operations were performing, Mr. Scott called in, accompanied by Jas. Taylor, Jr. of Zanesville who intended proceedg.—homewards this morning, and will, doubtless, call on you. I feel much indebted to his attentive kindness during my short stay in Cincinn. We went together to the office of the Literary Gaz. [Gazette] and afterwards to the P. O. where I saw Mr. Burke and Mr. Langdon, his asst. and deposited a letter which you will probably receive next Saty evg. Mr. Langdon accompanied me and introduced me to Mr. Wm. Bosson, a mercht. of Cincinn. who has lately returned from Harmony, where he has a brother—a member of the Community, to whom he gave me an introductory letter, and likewise to 2 merchts. in Louisville. Mr. B. also kindly introduced me to Messrs. Clark & Greene, agents for the Community. They offered me, & I accepted an introductory letter to Wm. Owen & likewise one to the Agents in Louisville. I spent *several hours* very agreeably in Mr. Bosson's store in conversation with him. He is a young man, very intelligent—apparently of an amiable disposition—

and devoted to the System. I learnt that Wm. Owen in the only member of his family now at Harmony—that his age is about 25, that the elder Mr. O. previous to his departure for Europe, called a meeting of all the members, in which mutual confidence was most strongly expressed. Mr. Owen dissolved the Committee appointed by himself, and requested the society to choose whomsoever they pleased—for some time this was declined, as all declared themselves well satisfied with his choice—but on being urged to it—they proceeded to the election; and the first person chosen was Wm. Owen. The greater part, if not all the other members were re-chosen. This is a pleasing mark of mutual confidence—another is, that Mr. Owen made an offer to the society of the whole establishment, land, buildings &c, at *their price own* and *on their own terms,* so well satisfied was he of their disposition and ability to carry the System into full & complete operation. Whether this offer was or was not accepted I did not learn, or have forgotten. It is certain, however, that things are going on well—the society has nearly overcome all the difficulties incident to such a heterogeneous congregation of strangers to each other. To my enquiry whether any new members cd. obtain admission, Mr. Bosson replied, that he thought no new families could as yet—but in *2 years,* the contemplated new village will be ready for the reception of members, as they are rapidly preparing materials. By the last accounts, the number of inhabitants amounted to 1050 or 1100. 370 children are daily taught in the schools—So far you will perceive I have heard nothing that has the least tendency to diminish my confidence in the System, either in principle or practice. On my arrival at Louisville, I shall close this letter, and put it into the Post Office there. At present I will only add that here I am again seated upright on the foot of my bed, my feet as before, resting conveniently on my foot board. I have cut the leather hinges of my provision box and the lid placed on my knees and covered with a towel forms a very convenient table for my meals—& writing. On the bed behind me are scattered my books and papers &c., &c., all very handy.—I write at my ease—without hurry or interuption—but after all—I would rather be seated in a comfortable house on shore, provided I hear not the tiresome question, "Is there any letter here for——". . .

Louisville, Sat. 13, Aug. 12 o'clock-noon.

We have just arrived here. The Capt. Finds it necessary to

unload almost entirely as he cannot pass the falls with more than 16 barrels of Flour—besides the winds ahead—I guess we shall not leave this place till noon tomorrow.

Unless something extraordinary occurs you will not hear from me again till I get to Mt. Vernon.

Ohio River 100 miles below Louisville.
Wed. 17 Aug. 1825.—

My dear William,

We reached Louisville last Saturday about noon, where I put a letter into the P. O. which you will probably receive next Tuesday evening. The Capt. immediately commenced unloading, and the boat passed the falls about sunset to Shippingport. In the meantime, I remained at Louisville & called on Messrs. I. & W. Stewart, agents for the Harmony Community, to whom I had a letter from Cincinnati. They have on hand a complete printing apparatus, (weighing about 2 tons) waiting an oppy. of forwarding it to Harmony. Here I regretted that our boat was so deeply laden that we could not take in on board. Here I also met with Mr. Larkin, a member of the Community, on his way down, with his famy—but excessively embarrassed how to contrive a conveyance. His report of affairs at Harmy [Harmony] which he left four weeks ago (to meet his famy—) corresponds exactly with all our previous information. I called at Dr. Galt's but had not the satisfaction of seeing him—his son (your former schoolfellow at Neef's) enquired particularly abt you. Next morning about Sunrise I set out to walk 2 miles to Shippingport & if the weather had been a little cooler shd have performed it with ease. Here I found them reloading the boat. Then I breakfasted & returned to Louisville to get some clothes I had left to be washed. When I returned to Shipt. the boat was reloaded, but everything so transposed, that I am not so conveniently located as before. However it matters little, for we shall be at Mt. Vernon next Saturday or Sunday. At Louisville I recd the O. R. [Ohio Republic] Aug. 6, the first I have seen since leaving Zanesville. The river is uncommonly low—we have had no rain but once—and that was of little or no service. We have left behind us everything we came in sight of—steamboats excepted.

I am writing this letter on board the boat intending, if possible, to put it into the P. O. at Troy, where we shall probably arrive tomorrow forenoon.

We started from Shippingport on Sunday afternoon abt 4

o'clock, and odd as it may appear to you, I was really glad to be on board again. I suffered excessively by the heat of the weather at Louisville and Shippingport, but here, I am comparatively comfortable—the greatest annoyance I now endure is from musketoes which have *begun* to be troublesome since we left Shippgpt. We no longer see any steamboats, though they were frequently passing and repassing us between Cincinn and Louisville.

The Capt. intends to write to Wm. Thompson from the mouth of the Cumberland river. In the meantime he requests you to say to him that he has ascertained the price of flour at Florence by a gentlemen who lately came from there, and who seemed desirous of buying him out at $5 per barrel which he declined. While at Louisville Mr. Boyd enquired of Wilson and Chambers, and likewise Buchanan, but they had no later accounts than about 4 weeks ago when flour was 6.50 to 7.00—their paper being at 10 per cent discount. He desires that you will apologise to W. T. for his not writing from Cincinn and Louisville, as he had not time, being very anxious to get forward. At Cincinn. he found a boat loaded with flour for Florence, which is left far behind.

From Mt. Vernon you may expect another letter from
   Your truly affectionate Father,
          Wm. Pelham.

      Mt. Vernon, Indiana.
      Mond. 22nd Aug. 1825.
      11 o'clock A.M.

This letter, my dear son, will apprise you of my arrival at this place, where I shall remain 2 or 3 days to recruit and refit, and then *take a walk* to New Harmony in co. [company] with a young man who resides there, and who will then return there.

The Post Boy landed me yesterday about 10 o'clock and I am lodging with Mr. Welburn, the Postmaster who is likewise agent for the new community. I have gained but little addition to me stock of information on the *interesting subject.* The young man alluded to is a carpenter & joiner—has been 3 months in Harmony—and is very well pleased with it.

The weather has, for the last 3 days been cloudy & *cold* and now threatens rain. I find that the E. [Eastern] mail arrives here every Monday, about noon, & immediately returns, crossing the river from, and recrossing to Kentucky & proceeding on that side to Louisville & Maysville. On Friday a mail is recd. from Vincennes & returns the same day through Harmony. You will hence perceive the most direct communication with this place and Harmony. * * *

After remaining here about an hour yesterday, Capt. Boyd proceeded on his voyage. He charged me $7—for my passage from Z. saying that this was $3 less that he would have charged if the agreement had been made at L. I find after all expenses paid *to this place*, I am just 18 dollars *minus* than when I started—and upon the whole, I am very well satisfied.

Remember me kindly to all friends. My next letter will be from N. Harmony.   Your affectionate Father,
Wm. Pelham.

[P. S.] By the bye, I have just learned from Mr. Wilburn that a printing press is actually in operation at Harmony though they have not yet commenced the publication of a newspaper.

New Harmony, Ind.
Th. 25 Aug., 1825.

My Dear William,
    I can only write you a few lines to say that I arrived here yesterday afternoon in company with a member of the community whose interesting information and conversation tended greatly to diminish the tediousness and fatigue of the *walk*. In a few days I shall write you again & at large.

Remember me kindly to all enquiring friends,
Yr affectn. father,
Wm. Pelham.

New Harmony, Inda. Sept 7, 1825.

My dear Son,
    I feel exceedingly desirous of writing to you, because I know a letter from me will be agreeable to you;—and yet I am loth to begin. Such a multitude of ideas crowd upon me, that I am doubtful whether I shall be able to select such as will be most interesting to you.

    I wrote you from Marietta—from Cincinn.—from Louisville—from Mt. Vernon— and lastly on my arrival here. At Mt. V. [Vernon] I settled with Absalom Boyd, the Capt. of the boat, and paid him $7 for my passage, baggage included, somewhat less than one cent per mile, which he assured me was, the usual rate.

After paying for the transportation of my baggage from Mt. Vernon hither $2—I found the $25 I had appropriated to the expenses of my journey almost exhausted. But here I am, without having experiences any disaster or serious inconvenience; having enjoyed uninterrupted health till a few evenings ago when I took cold by incautiously exposing myself to the night air. I am now again as well as before.

At Mt. Vernon I was introduced to Mr. Schnee, a member of the Committee, and Postmaster here, on his return from Shawneetown on business of the Society. We soon became acquainted, and it appears that we were mutually pleased with each other. His countenance and manner indicated good sense, good nature, and firmness of character, and on further acquaintance I find these indications were not fallacious. He is an intelligent, active, viligant, and efficient member of the Committee. He left Mt. Vernon the day before I did and met me at the Tavern in Harmony on my arrival. After I had taken some refreshment, he conducted me to the Committee room, and introduced me to Mr. Wm. Owen, Mr. Secretary Lewis, Mr. T. M. Bosson, Mr. Jennings and Dr. McNamee, all members of the Commee, by whom I was severally greeted with kindness unalloyed by affectation or ostentation. I soon discovered that forms and ceremonies have no place here, and the intercourse being plain, easy and free, is exactly suited to my taste. Plainness of manners and plainness of dress are characteristic of this society.

I lodged two nights at the Tavern, and then removed to the room I now occupy and in which I am now writing. It was offered to me by Mr. Bosson, being an unfinished one immediately above his own, which is scarcely any better, but they will do for the present, and as the cold weather advances we shall have to shift our quarters or be frozen to death. These rooms are in the house where the meetings of the Committee are held, and the only difference is, that the Comee rooms are lathed and plastered. Within two-hundred yards of us stands the Old Harmony church, a large frame building painted white with a steeple containing a clock which strikes the hours and quarters. By this clock are regulated the occupations and amusements of the inhabitants. At five every morning the bell is rung for the commencement of the daily business, at seven it is again rung to signify that breakfast will be ready in all the boarding houses and the Tavern in a qr. [quarter] of an hour. At 12 it is rung again & dinner is ready everywhere in fifteen minutes, the same at six for supper. Every

Tuesday evening such as chuse to dance assemble in the Hall (which is a large brick building near and almost adjoining the church) where they find an excellent band of music, and amuse themselves till nine o'clock. The utmost order, regularity and good humor exist here and I have witnessed these periodical dancing assemblies with approbation and pleasure, the music being excellent.

On Wedy, evg. such of the society as choose to attend in the church are made acquainted with the transactions of the Comee —during the preceding week, and everyone gives his opinion freely respecting the best course to be pursued. On Thursday evg. there is a regular concert, on Friday something else which I do not recollect and Saturday evening is not appropriated to any particular object. On Sunday the Rev. Mr. Jennings commonly delivers a lecture in the forenoon (without any formal text) in which he explains the manner of receiving religious impressions. I have not yet heard one of these Sunday lectures, but from several conversations I have had with him, I can plainly see that he will never try to stupify the understanding of his hearers with unintelligable dogmas, and incomprehensible jargon. What he says is plain, and easy to be understood. On the Thursday, that is, the next day following my arrival, a Baptist preacher came into the town and announced his intention of delivering a discourse in the evening in the Church. Accordingly, a large congregation assembled, and listened to him with great attention. He is certainly one of their first rate preachers, and he managed his matters with much address. The next evening—(Friday) Mr. Jennings delivered a lecture in the same place, and ably demonstrated the sandy foundation of the ingenious gentleman's arguments, without any pointed allusion to him or his arguments. At the close of the lecture my gentleman thought proper to make a rejoinder, tho nothing had been said of him or his doctrines, but he did not seem to be in so good a humor as he was the evening before—although he had previously preformed the marriage ceremony for a young couple—especially when this young couple retired with their friends into the *Hall* to enjoy the pleasures of music and dancing instead of listening to his rejoinder.

I have now been here 2 Sundays. On the first (Mr. Jennings being absent on business) Mr. Wm. Owen read to the congregation some extracts from his fathers publications—and last Sunday, Mr. Jennings being indisposed, another member read several extracts from other portions of Mr. Owen's works. In both instances these extracts were accompanied with appropriate remarks of the reader explaining and connecting the passages. Last Sunday *afternoon* we were regaled with a truly *christian* harangue from a rambling shaking quaker who happened to be here.

You would be surprised to see how punctually I attend these Sunday meetings in the Church, and how frequently I am perambulating the streets, and falling in and conversing familiarly with successive groups *before the door of the Tavern* particularly in the evening when these groups commonly assemble—not to drink and carouse, but for the purpose of rational conversation, here are no brawling braggarts, no idle jesters delighting to wound the feelings of each other—no intemperate buffoons eager to make sport of one another, for no member of the community can obtain any ardent spirit either at the Tavern or the store, without a certificate from the Doctor that it is needed as a medicine—a regulation that would be very useful in Zanesville as well as here. I have mixed much with all descriptions of persons, and I declare I have not heard an offensive word spoken by a single individual. Good humored jokes are undoubtedly frequent but the general tenor of the conversation is of a serious philosophical cast. Those who are incapable of this appear still to take an interest in discussions of this kind, or separate into groups to talk over the occurrances of the day, occasionally introducing some jocular remark, tending to excite mirth without wounding the sensibility of any.

As to dollars & cents, they are words seldom heard any where but in the public store, which is like all other trading shops, differing however in this, that every head of a family, or single unmarried member unconnected with a family, instead of carrying money to the store, is furnished a Pass-book in which he is charged with what he buys, and is credited every week with the amount of his earnings. These pass-books exhibit a curious medley of items, bacon, chickens, eggs, melons, cucumbers, butter, tea, sugar, coffee &c &c with all the varieties of *store goods* on the debit side, while on the other are placed the credits of the individuals. I have been several days employed in overhauling and balancing these pass-books (the clerk whose particular duty it is, being sick) and this has given me the opportunity of making these observations, which indeed anyone may do who will take the trouble of looking over them, for they are open to the inspection of all who choose to examine them. There are about 300 of these pass-books continually in motion.

At the particular request of Mr. Keightly and Mr. Harris, I have obtained the insertion of their names in the register of applicants for admission into the Society, and if they were now here, I have no doubt they would both find immediate employment, the former in the Turners' & machine makers shop appertaining to the Steam mill, the latter in the Pub. [public] store; But they would certainly be puzzled to find comfortable lodgings especially if they did not come prepared with a sufficiency of bedding and utensils for housekeeping. If any other of our friends wish me to have their names also inscribed in the Register, I will make application for them, on their request being made known to me—the notification must contain the name and age of the applicant, the age of his wife, if a married man—the number, ages and sexes of his children—the place of his birth, and his present residence—his trade or occupation—and his motive for wishing to join the society.

The manner in which I became employed in the Pub. [public] store was this. As no one in this community is urged or pressed to perform any work that he pointedly dislikes, it was delicately intimated to me by the Accountant at the store that the young man whose duty it was to attend to the pass-book department being sick his business was running behind and my services wd be acceptable *as long as I liked to continue them.* Notwithstanding my aversion to commercial matters I readily assented and entered the Counting room, where I *at once* found myself *at home*, though among strangers—such is the frankness of manners prevailing here. I would, however, rather be somehow or other connected with the printing establishment, and I think I shall accomplish this as soon as the publication of the paper is commenced. I have frequently conversed with Mr. Palmer the superintendent of the pr. [printing] office who has already in some instances accepted my services as corrector of several proof sheets of a pamphlet he is printing. I have been urging on the Comee. to commence the publication and I think it will commence next week, probably on Saturday the 7th inst. I shall not fail to forward it to you for exchange. You will of course send yours & if the Reformer is *not* printed in Philad. let me know where it is printed.

Mr. Schnee informed me yesterday that the mail route from hence is to Princeton—from thence to Evansville, and so along on the Indiana side of the river to New Albany where it crosses over to Louisville, thence to Cincinn. or Maysville, he is not sure which, but most probably to Cincinn.

And now, my dear Wm. I hope you will give me a letter at least once each week, letting me know how you all go on & especially if you meet with any Post Office difficulties. Never mind John Dillon or his ill-humor abt the newspapers, but make him pay his postage. One thing I particularly recommend & that is *to exact punctual payment* from *all* for fear of the worst. * * *

Yr aff. father,

Wm. Pelham.

N. Harmony, Sept. 8, 1825.

My dear Wm. * * *

You will perceive by my letters to the P. M. G. and to Dr. Bradley that I have become a Harmonite and mean to spend the remainder of my days in this abode of peace and quietness. I have experienced no disappointment. I did not expect to find every thing regular, systematic, convenient—nor have I found them so. I did expect to find myself relieves from a most disagreeable state of life, and be able to mix with my fellow citizens without fear or imposition—without being subject to ill humor and unjust censures and suspicions—and this expectation has been realized—I am at length *free*—my body is at my own command, and I enjoy mental liberty, after having long been deprived of it. I can speak my sentiments without fear of any bad consequences, and others do the same—here are no political or religious quarrels, though there is a great diversity of opinion in matters of religion. Each one says what he thinks, and mutual respect for the sentiments of each other seems to pervade all our intercourse. Mr. Jennings is *our* preacher, and I hear him with approbation and satisfaction. The Methodists have likewise a preacher among them, who sometimes holds forth to the great delight of those who take pleasure in confounding their understanding. I am in habits of intimacy with Mr. Jennings, and Mr. Bosson particularly, who are both men of great powers of mind I am on the best terms with Mr. Schnee, who I may even venture to call my friend, and likewise with the other members of the Committee.

I heartily wish you were here—you would at once find employment in the printing office, and pass your life hapily—You would be associated with a number of young men who form a band of music, and perform a concert every Thursday evg. You would even, join in the *dance* which takes place once a week. Your military propensities would be fully gratified in finding a sufficient number of congenial dispositions who are fond of that pursuit and have formed themselves into a Co. of St. Infantry under the direction of Capt. Larkin, who takes pleasure in it. They have just recd. their uniform from Pittsburg, but have not yet appeared in it. Upon the whole, after a full comparison of the advantages and inconveniences of my present situation I am quite satisfied. Let us now attend to other matters. * * *

There has for some time past been a good deal of conversation and consultation about establishing a social, circulating library, but nothing has yet been decided on. Whenever this is determined on I am to be Librarian, which, with my occupation in the printing office will be sufficient employment for me—and of the most agreeable kind—and with agreeable people. You may be sure I am doing all I can to bring it about. In the meantime I spend my time in obtaining a correct knowledge of the local affairs of the place. In due time I will communicate the result of the observations I may be able to make. At present I am boarding with the only baker in the town at 57 cents per week. He is a young married man—no children—and our dinner party consists of himself, his wife—Mr. Bosson and myself. That is, Mr. B. and I have our breakfast—dinner and tea there—and our lodging as before described, so that I may say, upon the whole I am very well situated.

I wish you would write me a long letter,—freely & confidentially, which will not fail to impart great satisfaction to, my dear Wm.   Yr. truly affectionate father,

Wm. Pelham.

New Harmony, Inda. Friday Sept. 9, 1825.

My dear William.

Yesterday evening, after I had written, sealed and put into the P. O. 2 packets directed to the "P. M. Zanesville" * * * , I received your acceptable favor of the 15th of August, accompanied with the O. Rep. of Aug. 13.

Associations on Mr. Owen's principles I find are springing up in the various places. Beside the society at the Yellow Spring, and the one you mention in Allegany Co. Pa. another has been formed at Albion, Illinois, the settlement made by the late Mr. Birkbeck, of which a favorable acct. has been recd. here.

Your information that Mess. Keightly and Harris will not

visit this place till October or November corresponds with what I learnt from themselves, and really I do not know how they will contrive to obtain accomodations when they do come. If they remain at the Tavern while they are not members they will be charged, each, $2 a week, as the Tavern is considered one of the sources of revenue for the society. If they come determined and prepared to join the society immediately, I think Mr. K. may manage to fit up some vacant log-hut for the reception of himself and famy. and Mr. H. might find admission into one of the boarding houses established for the accommodation of members of the community. It was fortunate for me that I had the precaution to bring all my bedding, tho upon opening my packages I was disappointed to find no thin coverlet. I really thought a white quilt had been put into the barrel or the large trunk. Your run was of great service to me. On board the boat it saved my bed and blankets from dirt & here it is tacked on the frame of my cob-bedstead. * * *

While at Mt. Vernon I heard the most unfavorable accounts of this place, but knowing how prone mankind are to speak ill of everything *intended for their benefit,* I paid but little attention to what was said. On my arrival here, the mystery was explained. The most bitter denunciators of the system were precisely those who applied for admission and been refused; because they were *idlers,* whose sole object was to be supported by the industrious part of the community. They were disappointed and hence arose their enmity. This society has certainly commenced under the most unfavorable circumstances. Their predecessors left everything to be *renewed*—before this establishment could be made productive. They settled themselves here in poverty and misery and departed in wealth and comfort, and considering these and other circumstances, it is rather surprising that their successors, coming from all quarters of the world, and unacquainted with one another's habits and dispositions, have been able to effect so much as they have done for their mutual convenience and comfort. Everyone with whom I converse, expresses the utmost confidence in the integrity, wisdom, and benevolence of Mr. Owen, and the day of his return will be a day of rejoicing throughout the settlement. The present Committee is composed of men of first rate ability—but they cannot perform impossibilities—they cannot in a day or a month change long established habits and prejudices, there must be time **for this,** and three months intercourse has already produced **much more** harmony of mind and unity of action than any other system is capable of producing. On my way from Mt. Vernon, within three miles of this place, I came to an extensive brick yard on the side of the road where a number of men were busily employed in making bricks for the new village, the location of which will be on the opposite side of the road.

You mention that you have "heard some discouraging news from New Harmony, propagated by an English ropemaker who left Cincinn quite charmed with the system, and has since returned disgusted." I have enquired into this matter and learned that the person alluded to, as soon as he came in sight of the town from the neighboring hills, declared that he was utterly disappointed and disgusted, he, nevertheless, came into the town—had all the talk to himself—tarried one night and departed next morning to enlighten his hearers on the subject of Mr. Owen's System for ameliorating the condition of mankind. How little could this man know of what he could so flippantly *talk about*,— and what sort of hearers must those people be, who could swallow his crudities?

Sunday Sept. 11, 12 o'clock M.

I have just returned from *Meeting;*—and strange as it may appear to you, I am a *constant attendant.* The orator was Mr. Jennings; and the substance, and indeed the whole of his discourse was a *moral lecture,* in the plainest and most intelligible language. He began by reading an extract from Robert Dale Owen's "Outline of the System of Education at Lanark" beginning at the 1st page, in which the author disclaims all necessity for reward or punishment in the education of children. The orator then proceeded to illustrate by familiar examples, the beneficial results of a course in which rewards and punishments are exploded, and the pernicious effects of an opposite course. Mr. Jennings then expatiated on the rights and duties of men in society, clearly showing that equality is the parent of liberty and justice; without a full enjoyment of which, mankind cannot be otherwise than unhappy. The discourse, as far as it could be regarded in a political light, was a truly democratic lecture, exhibiting the ill consequences arising from artificial distinctions, in station, in dress, and appearance and recommended as much uniformity in these particulars as may be practicable in this preliminary society. At the close of the lecture he announced that the publication of the "New Harmony Gazette" would be commenced on next Saty. week—viz. the 24″ of Sept.

I learnt today that the Committee determined yesterday that the publication of the paper should commence under the direction of Mr. Jennings and Mr. Owen & that my assistance would be acceptable as Corrector &c &c.

Tuesday evg., 13th.

Yesterday morning Mr. J. conducted me to the *Editorial room* which is a commodius one in the house where he resides. * * * Here I commenced my operations by filing, *at my leisure,* all the newspapers in possession of the establishment, consisting chiefly of the N. Intelln. [Intelligence] & N. Journal and of these not many. Mr.J. has a good, tho small collection of books which he has placed in this room.—

Now while I think of it, I will tell you what would be acceptable to me if Mr. Keightly could make it convenient to take charge of them when he comes in November.

1st. All the books &c on the enclosed list. Of the others, retain what you please, and send me the remainder.

2dly. My bedstead which I left standing in the front room and if accompanied with a sacking bottom—the old curtains and valance—so much the better. I can have a tester made here.

3rd. An old quilt of some sort, and a hammer to drive *small* nails, tacks &c.

4th. Four chairs which I left in the front room.

5. The looking glass which hung in the back parlor in the mahogany frame. If I had been certain of remaining here when I left Z. I should have brought these things with me, for I am daily experiencing the want of some of them.

Wed. 14 Sept.

At 4 o'clock this afternoon I shall have been here 3 weeks, having arrived on the 24th Aug. as stated before, and really I seem already to be an *old inhabitant,* which I can no otherwise account for than by the circumstance of my having become acquainted with so many people and the frank and friendly intercourse subsisting among us. Whatever difference of opinion there may be, (and there is in reality a great difference in religious matters)—I hear no illiberal remarks, I see no overbearing temper exhibited, but each one pursues his own course without meddling with his neighbor. The most numerous sect, I believe, is that of the persons who take delight in wandering with Baron Swedenborg in the regions of fancy, where they are permitted to roam at large without annoyance or molestation. As they experience no persecution, they have nothing to complain of, only that others will not wander with them. The same remark applied to the other sectarians, and hence a kind of tacit agreement has been made to let each other alone. You can scarcely imagine how well satisfied I am with this state of things, so much I assure you, that no temptation could again draw me into the vortex of mental tyranny from which I have escaped. Liberty of speech and action without infringing on the rights of others, has ever been the object of my ardent desire, and here at length, I enjoy it.

Thursday Morning.

As I have nothing new to communicate respecting myself or others, I will endeavor to give you some idea of the buildings and general appearance of this place, premising that the town is laid off in squares, similar to Zanesville, though the houses and gardens are far from being as regular. There is a considerable number of brick houses, some frame buildings, and a great many log-cabins, some of which are built of hewed logs, the others round and rough. In the center stands the Church, near which is an excellent pump, at about an equal distance from the Church and Tavern. Mr. Rapp's large brick dwelling on one side fronts the Church, or rather the square in which the Church stands; and on the other, fronts the main street, having in each front 7 windows below and 7 in the second story. The boarding houses, and the boarding school the new church (now called the Hall) the steam mill, and the public store, are all of brick, and are more or less large, acording to their respective uses. The brick as well as the frame dwelling houses are built on an uniform and very limited scale, and none of them of more than 2 low stories, the ground floor being invariably as follows, with the gable end to the street & a small garden full of fruit trees attached to each. They are commonly placed at the corners of the squares. The workshops are mostly in log huts. The upper story is an exact counterpart of the lower one, if the lower rooms hold all the family the large upper room and the little cell over the kitchen are appropriated to boarders.

The log-cabins are scattered about without the least regard to regularity of location. The *situation* of this helter-skelter village is really beautiful, and since the surrounding land has been cleared and drained, is healthy. The town receives its supply of water for domestic use from a number of wells and pumps dispersed through it, and I understand it is of that kind called limestone. For washing the inhabitants depend on rain and river water.

I have been here three weeks & I have not yet seen the Wabash!! The reason is that I find so many other things attracting my attention that my rambles have been much circumscribed. In fact, my chief object has been to make myself acquainted with the individual character of the human beings by which I am surrounded, and the system of government in operation. I have now reason to believe that the principle care of providing matter for the N. H. [New Harmony] Gazette will devolve upon me and my time will consequently be engaged by that concern. Of the two members of the Committee who were appointed to superintend the press, Mr. Jennings has declined, in order that he may give his whole attention to the superintendence of the Boarding School & Mr. Owen's daily & pressing occupations leave him no time, so I think the paper will be left pretty much to Mr. Palmer and myself, with such *occasional* assistance as we can extort from the literati. Although the day fixed for the commencement of the paper of the 24" of this month, I do not like that it should be begun on that day, and as it has already been so long delayed I shall endeavor to postpone it *one week* longer that it may commence on the 1st of October. By this arrangement the 1st vol. will comprise 7 months ending on the 1st May, the 2nd 6 months ending on 1st Nov. and every other vol. 6 months ending alternatly on 1st Nov. and 1st May, the latter being the anniversary of the adoption of the New Harmony Constitution. Whether the Comee. will agree to the postponement I know not, but I shall urge it, with due diference. I have not mentioned it yet to Mr. Palmer but I have no doubt of his assent.

Since writing the above, I have conversed with Mr. P. [Palmer] on the subject. He says each year will form one vol. in the manner of the Cincinnati Literary Gaz. and other similar papers. * * *

Most truly yr affectionate father,

Wm. Pelham.

Monday 19 Sept. 1825.

Yesterday at 10 o'clock A. M. Mr. Jennings ascended the pulpit in the old Church (which is now called *The Church*) and continued the reading of Robert Dale Owen's Outline of Education. His auditors were about as numerous as usual. He again expatiated on the indispensable necessity of establishing the principle of equality as the basis of liberty. He showed the absolute necessity of everyone being diligent in the performance of his or her respective duty. He was listened to with profound attention, and the discourse he delivered must produce good effects because it was reasonable and perfectly intelligible to all.

At 2 o'clock P. M. it was announced by the ringing of the bell that something was to be said or done at church. I immediately repaired hither, and found the pulpit occupied by a stranger who thought he could say something that would be useful. Very few persons were present. The gentleman began by giving out a hymn to be sung by the congregation—only one person joined him. After hobbling through one verse, the remainder was laid aside and "Let us pray" pronounced in an audible voice. Some knelt down, some stood, and others remained sitting. The preacher delivered a devout prayer, and seemed much relieved by this effusion of the spirit. He then commenced an attempt to reconcile some contradictions in the holy book—and talked about $\frac{3}{4}$ of an hour in the usual, incoherent, unintelligible manner. I found afterwards that his remarks made little or no impression on his hearers.

At 8 p. m. the bell again rang and I again attended where I found a considerable number of persons assembled to hear a preacher of the Methodist doctrine whose name I could not learn, though I inquired of several persons. I found, however, that he was one of the Circuit preachers. This man appeared to have learned his lessons very accurately, for his cant phrases flowed from him with remarkable ease and rapidity, and were answered by many *spiritual groans*, and other evidences of entire sympathy. When he gave out a hymn, a considerable number of male and female voices were joined with his, and really the music was delightful, for singing is taught here scientifically. He then named a text, and talked as usual about sin, and the devil, and heaven, and the straight and narrow way leading to salvation, the utter impossibility of being saved but through the merits of our blessed Lord and Savior, Jesus Christ &c &c. I mustered patience to sit and hear him to the end and when the judge pronounces against me "Depart ye wicked &c" I intend to plead this command of myself in mitigation of the sentence. After he had finished, a member of the Community with whom I am acquainted, and who is a sort of a Methodist preacher, took his place in the pulpit, and in a moderate tone and manner related his individual experience as an example to others, he was also attended to though he said nothing but what had been said a thousand times. It seems he is unwilling to exchange his belief in divine revelation for all the joys and pleasures of the world.

So be it, for notwithstanding this whimsical notion, he is really a good member of the Society, and devoted to the system as far as he comprehends it.

You would be amused to come into the church while we are at our devotions. The walls bare—the ceiling lofty—the beams and joists uncovered, the pulpit itself nothing but a raised platform furnished with a bench, and sort of desk, the preacher in his ordinary clothing, a striped roundabout and linen pantaloons—(this is the common appearance of Mr. Jennings, Mr. Owen and some others) benches ranged for the congregation, on one side for the men, on the other for the females, many of the former in their shirt sleeves, among the latter a variety of ornamental drapery, and among the whole the greatest order and decorum. No one troubles himself about his neighbor's appearance unless there be an affectation of finical attention to dress. This however, will wear away gradually.

Tuesday evg. 9 o'clock.

I have just returned from the Hall, where there is music and dancing every Tuesday evening. Every Friday evening there is a concert in the same place. Some biggots are dreadfully scandalized that these parties are held in a building originally intended for divine worship, nevertheless, the fire and brimstone have not yet descended from heaven to destroy us for this wicked perversion.

Yesterday evening there was a drunken frolic among some young men who contrived to procure some whiskey from the country people who came in to make their purchases in the store. The Committee took cognizance of the matter today, and have expelled three of the offenders, who are deemed incorrigible, being not only addicted to drink but likewise gamblers and idlers. What sort of character will these men give us when they return to their homes?

It is now determined that the paper shall be published on the 1st of October, being the day Mr. Owen embarked in England 12 months ago, to come to America. I gave Mr. Palmer all the matter I had prepared for the first paper, and he said there was enough for 3 at least. The paper will be in 4to—the size of the Cincinnati Literary Gazette.

Tell Mr. Keightly that articles of provision will be in demand here in the course of the winter, such as hams, pickled pork, potatoes, and perhaps flour. Vegetables of all kinds are very scarce, for the old Harmonites left the garden fences in a wretched condition, and before they could be repaired by the new comers, the hogs and cows had very materially injured the gardens. Some persons think that Mr. Owen will not be here till the middle of December and I am much of the same opinion.

I have traversed the town to find a suitable editorial room in which I might place my bed, but hitherto without success. Many of the young men are lodging in barns and other out-houses, so that my present *shell* is esteemed a very confortable location, nevertheless I must have better winter quarters, or they will have me on the Doctor's list before Christmas. Of this, however, I have no great apprehension, for every member of the Committee seems disposed to accomodate me as well as circumstances will permit. * * *

Thursday Evg.

At this moment (half past eight) the moon is shining brightly and the light infantry company under Capt. Larkin, dressed in their new uniform (very much like yours) are marching and countermarching in the square and in the streets, accompanied by the boys under the direction of their respective school-masters who teach them to perform the same evolutions which they do with great precision.

This afternoon I attended the funeral of a female member. She was burried out of the town in a corner of a fine apple orchard, and without any of the parade and *cant* that I have formerly seen and heard on such occasions.

I must now quit writing and search 12 or 15 newspapers for matter to be inserted in the 1st number of the New Harmony Gaz. It is always best to take time by the forelock.

Tell Mr. Nims, Mr. Westbrook and Mr. Sheward and all others who may inquire of you that the want of accommodation here at present is so great that I would recommend to them if they seriously contemplate a removal hither to postpone it till they hear further from me. * * * Wm. Pelham.

Monday Evg. Sept. 26, 1825.

On Saturday evening last, the Society was called together by the Committee to decide a case, which, being the only one yet presented to their notice, the Committee did not choose to determine, on their own authority only. The case was this.

The Superintendent of the Steam Mill had at several times complained to the Committee, that his pay was not sufficient for the support of himself and his family. On such occasions, the Committee, conformably to their usual practice, gave him an additional credit at the store. By this means he became a debtor to the Society, under the presumption that he would continue a member, and gradually wipe off the debt. But it seems that this was not his intention; for, a few days ago, having obtained another order on the store to the amount of sixty dollars, and received the goods he wanted, he suddenly gave notice of his intention to withdraw from the society. On settlement of his account, the balance against him, after every allowance, was $77.62½ This balance he refused to liquidate in any manner whatever, and the members of the Society were summoned to determine what steps should be taken on this novel case. After much discussion and ample explanation on both sides, a large majority determined by vote, that the Superintendent restore so much of the property drawn from the store as could be restored, for which he should have credit, and that for the remainder of the debt he should give his note payable at a time to be agreed on, and further, that if he refused to comply with these terms he should be expelled.

I understand that the affair has been adjusted in some way, and that he will, tomorrow, retire from this place. During the meeting he endeavored to excite a spirit of general discontent among the members, but in this he utterly failed, and I have reason to believe that such attempts will always meet with a similar fate. I know not whither he is going, but doubtless, wherever he goes he will spread a doleful account of the injustice and oppression he experienced at New Harmony and advise his hearers to shun this place as they would a pleague or pestilence.

Yesterday at the usual hour, Mr. Wm. Owen ascended the *pulpit* in *the Church*, and read that portion of Robert Dale Owen's "Outline of Education" which treats of the subject of religion, with explanatory remarks and comments of his own. He is a good reader and speaker, except that his voice is not sufficiently strong and firm. His audience was numerous and attentive. His manner is most mild and conciliating, for he is an amiable young man, about twenty five. He only wants experience.

This afternoon, the weather being fine, I treated myself with a view of the Wabash; the distance from my lodging being but little more than a quarter of a mile to the landing. The river is beautiful, and at this place about half the width of the Muskingum at Zanesville. The shore is a sandy beach intermixed with small pebbles. The bank appeared to be about twenty feet high from the level of the water. From the foot of the bank to the edge of the water about the same distance. There were two or three boats lying at a little distance above the landing place.

Tuesday noon.

Last night the weather was so cold as to require a good fire. This coldness of the air silenced the musicians who have so diligently amused the inhabitants of this town every since I have been here. I mean certain little winged insects who take care to indemnify themselves for any trouble they are at to entertain us, by piercing the skin and drawing off the *superfluous* moisture. On my complaining of these troublesome visitors, I was told, "Never mind it,—you will get used to them"—and so indeed I found out; for I begin to be very indifferent about them. In reality, I have become inattentive to many inconveniences which would have worried me excessively in Zanesville. So much depends on the state of the mind.

Afternoon 4 o'clock.

I have just come from the printing office, where Mr. Palmer is working off one side of the paper. He has an elegant new Superroyal press of the kind called the Stansbury press, which requires less than one third of the strength necessary for working the common screw press. It cost $170. Having no knowledge in these matters, I cannot give you a description of it. I can only perceive that the labor of pulling the bar is comparatively nothing. I wish you had such a one, or that you were here to try the difference. * * *

As you have had the opportunity of seeing a great number of newspapers, I wish you would send me a list of such as you recommend in exchange, omitting all that you know to be violent party papers, such as Democratic Press, N. York Advocate, Richmond Enquirer, and others of the same stamp. What do you think of the Athens Mirror in this point of view? I think it is a literary paper and it is such we want. But we want not any of the canting, hypocritical, lying religious papers so called, which tell us everything but the truth and whose sole object is to "Milk the Goats."—If you don't understand this expression ask our friend, Martin Hill to explain it as he found it explained in "Plain Truth."

The superintendent alluded to in the beginning of this letter is gone, having previously restored some of the goods he obtained, and given his note for the balance, with acceptable security. * * *

My thoughts often dwell on you & and always with the feelings of
An affectionate father,
Wm. Pelham.

Private and confidential. Sept. 29. [1825]

What I have written to you, since my arrival here is strictly true as far as it goes, though I would not wish anything you receive from me *in manuscript*, to appear in the paper, unless I particularly request it. Many things are in an unsettled state, and will probably remain so till Mr. Owen's return.

As an instance—After Mr. Jenn. & Mr. O. were appointed by the Com. to superintend the press, I applied to them for matter, both original and selected. The former explicity declined, and threw the burden on me—& the latter was so immersed in his daily business that I could scarcely get an opportunity of speaking with him. I went on as well as I could, & prepared the matter, corrected the proof of the first side, & returned it to the printer. The form was worked off yesterday afternoon. This morning Mr. J. found several things which he said must be altered—but it was too late. This brought an explanation, and it is now determined, that an hour shall be appointed when they are jointly to attend to the business. This will be a great relief to me. At 2 o'clock this afternoon they did indeed meet at the Printing Off. accompanied with 2 other members of the Com. to revise the matter prepared for the inside of the paper—and cut down a good deal of the manuscript laid before them—whether for better or worse, I cannot determine. At all events they have done something, and the paper will be published according to appointment.—When once begun, it must go on—Mr. J. wrote a few lines to precede my biograph. sketch of Mr. O.—Mr. Bosson wrote the View of N. H. and the piece relating to the salubrity of this town & adjacent country—I wrote the head introducing the Song No. 1 and they say it ought to have been more full & explicit—but none of them presented this full & explicit statement.—I have mentioned these circumstances to show that we have *not yet* got into a regular train, though it will certainly, in 2 or 3 weeks, be established. I want Niles' Reg. to take his Summary of news. This will save time and trouble.

I have several times been present when Mr. Schnee opened his mail & have sometimes assisted. Tomorrow he is going to make up his quarterly accounts & he wants me to be with him tho' I know he can do it as well without as with me for he is an intelligent man of business. His Acct. of Mails Received will occupy 2½ pages.—Adieu!— [Wm. Pelham]

Monday Oct. 3, 1825.

My dear Wm. * * *

Friday evg. was a bustling time in the printing office. The paper was expected with great impatience by the town subscribers (who flocked in at $1 per ann.) besides whom a number were to be prepared for the E. [Eastern] mail which closes at 9 o'clock P. M. However we got through the business pretty well, as we have a set of people to deal with very different from the Zanesvillians or *Lunarians*, as they ought to be called. * * *

Yesterday morning I was prevented by circumstances from shaving and dressing myself till the second bell rung for meeting. I was unwilling to be absent and *finally* at the instigation of Wm. Owen I, determined to go as I was, viz. with a long beard, dirty shirt and cravat and my little short coat which is the coat I most commonly wear when the weather is warm.

Mr. Jennings began with reading something from a late publication on Political Economy, after which he delivered an excellent discourse on Equality:—shewing that it was essential to the happiness of society, as all arbitrary distinctions and partialities not founded on real merit, and all distinctions arising from extravagance in dress and external appearance have no solid foundation—that every person's worth should be measured by his capacity to be useful to his fellow beings. Many ladies were present, some of whom were fashionably dressed and decorated with ribbons and artificial flowers. I suspect that some of them did not quite approve of his remarks.

On Friday I changed my boarding house that I might be better situated in regard to my connection with the pr[inting] off[ice]. The house in which this office is located is also a boarding house, kept by Mr. Palmer, the printer. On one side of the office which is a large room on the ground floor a long table is placed at which the boarders (about thirty)—receive their meals which are punctually on the table at a quarter past 7 A. M. a qr. past 12 noon, and a qr. past 6 P. M. The price of boarding everywhere in town (except the Tavern) is 57½ cents per week for each person, being a member. This table is better supplied with butcher's meat and vegetables than the one I have just left, but not so well supplied with milk just now. You may easily imagine what a contract there must be between the talk and bustle of so many boarders, and that of the four persons which formed our meal parties at the baker's. The first day or two, I was almost stunned with the noise, but I am getting used to it. Another thing I am getting used to is the shrill note of the cricket in my bed room which I have *no possible means* of getting rid of. There are so many and such important circumstances to counterbalance the inconveniences I suffer that I may say "Upon the whole, I am very well satisfied."

Wednesday 5th.

Yesterday evening being the regular dancing evening a number of ladies appeared at the ball in a new *uniform* dress of cheap American manufacture. I was prevented from seeing this exhibition by having to read a proof-sheet which I did not get till after dark. As soon as I had performed this duty I sallied out with the intention of going to the Hall. As soon as I got out of doors I perceived that the Church also was lighted up, and as it lay in my way I called there first and found about twenty devotees listening to the ranting of a stranger who occupied the pulpit, and who was holding forth with great strength of voice about the "scribes and Pharisees." I did not sit down, and only remained a few minutes. Having heard as much about these gentlemen of the ancient world as I desired, I proceeded to the ball-room, but too late to gratify my curiosity with the sight of the new dresses.—The west door of the Church and the e [ast] door of the Hall are about 10 feet apart.—

My best wishes attend you all. Wm. Pelham.

P. S. The impression of No. 1 consisted of 500 copies of which 300 have been distributed to subscribers and others.

Monday 10″ of Oct. 1825.

Yesterday according to my *new* custom, I went punctually to Church, and heard Mr. Jennings continue the reading of select portions of Thompson's Essay on the distribution of wealth. The author shews distinctly, that a very considerable part of the evils suffered in Society may be traced to the unequal, and unjust division of property, and that this again may be attributed to the principle of individual competition. He then contrasts with this the social system, from whence this principle is banished, with all its train of evils, and the principle of mutual co-operation substituted with all its necessary consequences. After the reading, the male and female children of the society sung the song No. 2. If I can get the music I will send it to you. Mr. J. then expatiated on his favorite topics, equality, economy, and good feelings toward one another. At the close of the discourse, he was requested by one of the members to give notice that at 3 P. M. there would be *preaching* in the Church. This he readily did, and with due respect. Accordingly, as I understand, for I did not attend, the Revd. Mr. Slocum a Methodist preacher delivered a very edifying sermon, that is to say, a sermon full of words and phrases quite unintelligible both to the speaker and his hearers—all of whom have probably persuaded themselves that they fully *understand* as well as profess to *believe* such things. In the evening the weather being warm and clear, many were assembled as usual before the door of the Tavern, (which is a sort of Literary Exchange)— where, seated on chairs and benches, we discussed with mutual respect, and perfect freedom, the various ideas of religion entertained by each—and here we sat and talked of God, the soul, eternity, matter, spirit, &c. &c. (without thinking of anything to drink) till after the Tavern doors were closed, which is always done at 10 o'clock. * * *

Adieu, my dear Wm. and remember me kindly to all friends. I must now close and begin reading the proof of the inside of our No. 3.   Wm. Pelham.

P. S. A letter dated Aug. 7 has just been recd. from Capt. McDonald, a member of the Community who accompanied Mr. Owen, stating their arrival at Liverpool, and the expectation that they will be ready about the first of October to embark on their return.

New Harmony, Ind.
Friday, 21 Oct. 1825.

My dear Son,

My time, during the present week has been so fully occupied, that I had none left to continue my journal, though several little things have occurred which might be interesting to you—for instance the mustering and appearance of our Light Infantry company and their marching out of town 5 miles to the ground appropriated to this object according to law.

Yesterday I had the satisfaction of seeing Messrs. Keightly and Harris in good health and spirits after a journey of 14 days having left Zanesville on the 6th inst. * * * They have this morning been accepted by the Committee as members of the Society and consequently each will have his board at one of the boarding houses (or as they are here called Community houses) at the rate of 57½ cents a week. The wages, or pay, or allowance (call it what you will) is proportionately low so that it amounts to this simple fact, that whoever serves the Society faithfully and diligently whatever his occupation may be, gets his living and no more. If he has children they are also provided for; either by his labor or their own if capable of earning anything, but if not then they are provided for by the Community till they are capable of being useful. This is merely a hasty sketch which I will enlarge upon one of these days when I have more time. I can only add that if any man should come here to board, without doing anything deemed *useful*, he must make an individual agreement with the Committee, for we want no *idlers* of any description, and several persons of this sort have already been dismissed, and many more will find it expedient to retire, leaving behind them the best part of the present population, whom nothing could induce to abandon the pleasing prospects before them. * * *

Your truly affectionate father,
Wm. Pelham

[P. S.] I will again revert to Harris and Keightly. After introducing them to the Committee individually and collectively I went with them in search of board and lodging as they wished to leave the Tavern as soon as possible. After going about a good deal we found an unoccupied garret,—in one of the Community houses—similar to mine, that is to say, no ceiling but the outside roof, but better than mine both in extent and walls, theirs being brick, and mine merely a *shell* of weather boarding. Without actual experience, one cannot realize the difficulty of getting house-room in this place. K [eightly] with his warm zeal is satisfied with his location and all concomitant inconveniences and privations. H [arris] is not quite so well contented, but as soon he begins to experience the beneficial change he has made as respects *Society*, he will be as well satisfied as any of us. A double feather bed has been procured—Keightly will make a bedstead—the store will furnish him with a bed cord—blankets must be had somehow. Keightly will be or is already I believe attached to the carpenter's shop and Harris will on Monday next be employed in the counting room at the store.

[P. S.] This is Tuesday night (Oct. 25th) warm and rainy. After supper, (the time of which is uniformly 6 o'clock) I called at the Tavern to see K [eightly] and H [arris]. They were both gone to the ball * * * . I then came home to my lodging, and here I am in my shell, surrounded by boards, carpenters' tools, shavings, sawdust &c. for the Committee, on my proposing to them the alternative of burying me, or making my room *comfortable* this winter very readily embraced the latter alternative and gave me the command of the carpenter's department so far as this was necessary for wood-work. I am also to have bricks, bricklayers &c. to fill in between the studs, and I have now a certain prospect of being very commodiously situated during the winter exactly in the location which of all others I prefer, for I should very reluctantly quit the quarters I have occupied ever since my arrival here. * * *

Thursday Morning.

Mr. Keightly has just called to inform me that he and Harris have concluded to return immediately to Zanesville. He will take charge of this letter accompanied by a pamphlet just warm from the N. Harmony Press. I beg you will read and study it. They are not yet made up. I shall endeavor to send you more copies in sheets for sale 25 cents each.

November 7", 1825, Monday.

My dear Son,

* * * You enquired how my postage acct. is settled here, I answer that all unpaid letters are charged in my pass book among other charges. In the same book I have credit for my services at——per week. I have yet said nothing about the rate of allowance, but suppose it will be $1.54 per week, this being the allowance to each member of the Comee. Soon after my arrival I deposited in the store $10 & have this day made an additional deposit of $20—both sums being credited to me in the books of the store as well as in my pass-book. These deposits have left me $7—which I still have in cash. I have taken up articles & pd for work $10.36—The pamphlets I sent you by Keightly are likewise charged in my pass-book and also $1.50 for which I became responsible to Mr. Pearson for work done for Messrs. Harris & Keightly while they were here & which was forgotten in the hurry of their departure. By this sketch you will see that my funds decrease but slowly. * * * Nor do I believe that any temptation *whatever* could induce me to quite this tranquil scene.

If I suffer inconveniences here they are accompanied with such alleviating circumstances as greatly deminish their effect.

I cannot help again reiterating the advice I gave you to come here as soon as possible * * *. There is a great number of young persons here of both sexes in this place, and I plainly see that they enjoy themselves and the society of each other, their labor is moderate and easy, and their recreations frequent and innocent. In short they please themselves, and generally if not always please one another. * * * You are aware, that reading written accounts of the circumstances of any place cannot supply the place of actual inspection. In order to form an accurate judgment you must actually see it, and converse *on the spot* with intelligent residents. K [eightly] & H [arris] have been here, the former is too flighty and his stay too short to form a distinct perception—and the latter is too querulous to be happy any where, for every place has its inconveniences and his temper of mind leads him to *dwell* upon these and overlook the counterbalancing advantages. Besides the poor fellow was tormented with a boil which entirely deprived him of whatever comfort he might otherwise have enjoyed. There is not a shadow of doubt in my mind that after five or six month's residence here it would be an exceeding difficult matter to induce you to remove elsewhere, and more especially to Z [anesville.] You may call this *enthusiasm*, if you please, but the real differences between this place and Z. will still exist in all their force, and certainly you must allow me to be a tolerable judge of them, from my having resided in both. The approaching winter will doubtless bring its additional inconveniences, and so will the spring, and so will the following summer, the chief of which is the want of house room.

I am now sitting (Tuesday night 11 o'clock.) in my room which has lately been filled in with brick and otherwise rendered a comfortable dwelling and my prospects during the ensuing winter are almost wholly agreeable. * * *

Respecting an establishment like this there must necessarily be a great variety of opinions and sentiments, and predictions, but you will find that those who have given the *least* attention to the subject are the *most* confident in prophesying its dissolution. Let them say what they will, you may feel *assured of its permanency*, and it is the unqualifies opinion of every intelliegent man here. For my own part, I have not the least doubt that the present inconveniences will gradually be supplanted by circumstances tending to promote and perpetuate the happiness of those who embrace the System.

           Wed. Morn. 11 o'clock.

 Smart frost last night. Weather now moderate & pleasant. I have just retd. from printg. O. 218 steps from thence to the door of my lodging * * *. There are no settled preachers of the Gospel here—but traveling preachers very frequently call and refresh the flock with the words of grace.

 With regard to the new village all that I can say is that the brickmakers—I know not how many—are constantly employed in preparing that material.

       New Harmony, Sunday Nov. 27, 1825.
My dear son.

 * * * I shall now endeavor to answer all the questions in your last letter, tho it contains some that I think were anticipated in my last. When I said "whoever serves the society faithfully and diligently, whatever his occupation may be, gets his living and no more" I meant that all ideas of individual wealth are banished from among us. If any chooses to earn more than his individual expenses, the surplus profits remain in common stock to be appropriated by the whole Society in whatever manner they please, for the good of the whole. This community being established on the principle of equal benefits and enjoyments, it is obviously different from our former plans of accumulating *wealth* for *individual* expenditure. Every one will enjoy an equal share with every other member, of the immense benefits produced by mutual cooperation. That this will be the ultimate effect of the System I have not the least doubt, though at present it is not exactly so, because it is impossible in the circumstances of the present establishment. You can hardly expect that in the heterogenous population hastily collected here, there shd be no idlers, no speculators &c, the most effectual measures are however in active operation to make a just discrimination and the certain effect will be the withdrawal or expulsion of those who came here to live upon the labors of others. This *preliminary* society cannot be considered as a fair sample of the perfect community in view, because it consists of persons differing much from each other in their tempers and inclinations, whereas the new community will consist of select characters actuated by feelings of *common interest*.

 At present there are many wants that cannot be *immediately* provided for, and the greatest of these is the want of suitable accommodation. For this reason the twenty persons you mention as coming from Pittsburg will have to retrace their steps, there is actually not house room for them. *Keep it in mind, however, that my room is large enough for us both.* All the conversations I heard in Zanesville, and the letters I have recd. since about this place relate to *pay*. In fact, no one here talks about *pay*. The Committee in their endeavor to equalize the members fixed the allowance of credit to each at 80 dollars a year which it was supposed wd be sufficient for his maintenance—but the principle, the main principle is that every grown person is able to earn his living, and if he feels disposed to earn more, the surplus, after every reasonable expenditure for individual comfort to every member is applied to the extension of similar establishments. This is the ultimate view—but the immediate object is for each member to do all he can to provide a fund from which he in common with others will derive all the enjoyments he requires, and it is *calculated* that a very moderate portion of labor will be abundantly sufficient for this.—

You want to know how the acct. stands between Mr. Owen & the Society. It is simply thus: Mr. Owen has advanced his own money for the purchase of this property. Just before his departure he made an offer of it to the Society on *their own terms*, which they declined, preferring that it should still continue to be his. He is therefore evidently sole proprietor of the whole; but it is equally evident that it will ultimately be the property of the whole Society, and that, as soon as the individuals find themselves competent to conduct the concern on the principles which brought them together. They have ever since his departure been endeavoring to make such arrangements as to produce the benefits in contemplation. Most of these plans have succeeded, but some have also failed, for the want of requisite practical knowledge. A general sentiment prevailes that *"things will go on better soon after the return of Mr. Owen"* who, it is expected will be here in a week or ten days. It would surprise you to hear the universal expression of the fullest confidence in the wisdom and integrity of Mr. Owen—he is certainly a most extraordinary man or he could never thus have attached him— to him so great a variety of characters as compose this population without a dissenting voice, as far as I know. This is not blind enthusiasm in me for I know the fact, and I know the greater part of these people have been *personally acquainted* with him. When *I* see him you shall have the result of my cool, candid observation.

"If a person joins, and invests, say $500—when he shd wish to retire can he get his cash again?" This is one of your questions. I read it to Mr. Lewis the Secretary of the Committee. He immediately answered "Yes, certainly!" "Does he draw interest?" "No Mr. Owen does not want to borrow." When a person retires who puts nothing into the common stock whatever balance may be due to him for his time & labor will be paid to him in the products of the establishment—the profits arising from his labor, *if any*, will be merged in the common stock, for the benefit of those who remain. It is not an easy matter to ascertain *profits*, in fact, there is no profit till the article manufactured be sold, and the money actually received. "Is there any chance for another butcher?" Not immediately; unless he could sleep in a hay loft.— "Should John Sockman join, what would he have to do?"—"and what *pay*?" We know nothing about *pay*. It is a term used only among you of the old world, and confined wholly to the selfish, *individual* system. Every one here who employs himself usefully has meat, drink, lodging—(when it can be got)—and is continually increasing his comforts. If sick he receives the necessary attendance. If he has children they are provided for. We have so saddler, nor is there any place for one to lodge in. This is a general answer to all inquiries and will continue so until some houses can be built. * * * "I do not at all like the account you give of your lodging room." My last letter will have informed you that it is not quite comfortable, tho still somewhat inferior to the *front room* &c. Everybody who comes into it exclaims *"How comfortably you are fixed here."* "How does the new village come on?" Not so fast as we wish, but as well as can be expected. The brickmakers have been at work *on the spot* during the whole summer and have made 240,000.

The dismal story you copied from the Pittsb[urg] Mercury was already known here, and the writer is also known. He is a Baptist preacher I heard him preach just after my arrival, and he went away displeased because Mr. Jennings out-preached him. I wd recommend to you to read in the Gazette if you want to know the truth of things—read the "View of Harmony." The Labyrinth has not been destroyed, but it has been neglected as of little comparative importance. * * * "What are the hours of business, summer and winter?" I am not sure about the working hours. The bell rings at six o'clock in the morning, but I believe few persons go to work till the eight o'clock bell rings. From this hour they continue till the 12 o'clock bell, at 1 the bell again **rings** and the working hours continue till 6 when the supper bell is rung. There is no job work—i.e. no person is paid by the job. When jobs are done in any department for country people or strangers— the superintendent of the department receives the cash and pays it into the store, and the department (be it the printing, tailoring, shoemaking &c department) is credited for the amount. * * * The "parade ground appropriated by law." This was an inadvertance of mine—the law does not appropriate any parade ground The general muster is held at a place five or six miles from hence, and all our *military* marched to that spot on the day appointed— this was what I ought to have said. Apropos—Our Light Infantry Co. & some other companies in full uniform are now, (Sund[ay] afternoon,) parading in the street under the command of their Major the Revd. Mr. Jennings, who is an active and intelligent military officer—He preached in the forenoon in the Church, and this afternoon appeared on horseback in his military dress to exercise the troops. The L. I. Co. make a good appearance being all properly armed, accoutred, and uniformed, they number about 40 all young men. * * *

You wd probably like to know how we go on with the paper. I therefore add to this long letter a few items on that subject. On the 20th inst. we reconed 116 Subd. in town at $1, the *members* being charged only half price. 4 sent to the Reading Room. 2 to the Tavern and 1 to the Committee, making 123 delivered in town. 175 forwarded by mail to Sub. and Prs. viz.

Pennsylvania	11s.	7 prs.	Conn.		1s.	1 pr.
Indiana	27s.	5 prs.	Ill.		20s.	1 pr.
Kent'y	7s.	3 prs.	Maryl'd		1s.	4 prs.
Mass	3s.	1 pr.	Delaware		1s.	1 pr.
Missouri	3s.		Tennessee		4s.	
Maine	1s.					
N. York	7s.	4 prs.	Scotl'd & Eng		6s.	1 pr.
Ohio	15s.	14 prs.	Virg'a		1s.	1 pr.
D. Col	8s.	4 prs.	N. Jersey		2s.	1 pr.
N. Carol		1 pr.	Louisiana		1s.	1 pr.
Mississi	1s.		Alabama		1s.	

2 Reading rooms at Cincinnati, 1 at Louisville, Alegheny and Y. Springs associations 2, total, 298. Since the 20 inst., 15 new subscribers abroad have been added to the list & every mail brings some. Papers recd. last Thursday were:

Reformer, Crisis, Ohio Repub. Nov. 2, Niles Reg. Times, Chillicothe, Ohio; State Jour. Col. Louisville Advertr., Dayton Repub., Vevay Regr., Hamilton Advocate, Marietta Friend, Athens Mirror, Lancaster O. Eagle, with a request fr Mr. Detrich of exch. addressed to me, Cleaveland Herald,

Ind. Repub., Madison, Vincennes W. Sun, Balt. Gazette, Balt. Dutch Paper, Delaw. Watchman, Wilmingtonian, Alb. Patriot, Traveller Boston, these are all addressed to the Gaz.—Cincinn also sends us Lib. Hall & N. Repub., Bloomington, Ind. Gazette, Georgetown Sentinal. These are all directed to the Gaz. besides which the followg. directed to individual: N. Intell., N. Journal, Wash. Metropolitan, Geo. T. Sat. Evg. Post, Globe and Emerald, Boston Cent, U. S. Gaz. daily.

The day of publication is changed to Wednesday which is a more convenient time than Saturday. News is a secondary object, the first being to disseminate a correct knowledge of the principles, practice, and local affairs of this Society. Wm. Owen appears to me to possess a better knowledge of the principles than any other person here, and his pieces are therefore the most interesting. His 2 articles in the 2 papers No. 7 & No. 8 preceding the last on the formation of character are peculiarly so. * * *

I wish you would frequently insert in the O. Rep. some extracts from the N. H. Gaz. particularly the editorial remarks in No. 7 & 8 on the formation of character, with any other selections calculated to excite the minds of your readers to the exercise of their *reasoning* faculties. The world has been long enough and too long under the dominion of passion and prejudice, and it is time that REASON shd have fair play. Perhaps while I think of it, I cannot give you a more striking illustration of the principles and practice of this Society than by citing Mr. Schnee as an example, he is Postmaster, Committee-man, Superintendent of the farms, and principle agent in the *selling* department of the store, and yet his *nominal* allowance in money is $1.54 per week for all his services put together. If he takes a boarder, 64 cents a week (it has lately been a little increased)— is added to his credit, and charged to the boarder. He has a wife and two or three sons, two of whom are capable of earning something which is also added to their joint credit unless they choose to have separate pass-books. They occupy a snug dwelling house, yard and garden, and find their allowance sufficient for their maintenance because they are all frugal and industrious. If they were to determine on a removal, their pass-books would be closely and critically examined in the Committee. If it appeared that they have been prudent and economical and a balance still exists against them further allowance will be made, so as to balance the acct, on the principle that the services of every industrious, prudent man are equal to the necessary expenses of his living. If on the contrary it should appear that they came here to speculate on the industry of others by running in *debt at the store* for articles not necessary but merely to accumulate property or indulge idle fancies, whatever balance there might be against them would be rigidly exacted in money or labor. This is evidently a just and necessary precaution against subjecting the better part of the society to the impositions of scheming speculators who might otherwise come here with the view of staying a few months, accumulating property at the expense of the industrious whom they leave behind them after having unworthily enjoyed all the advantages of membership. Some cases of this kind have occurred and the parties have gone away, highly displeased with the Society, because they were disappointed in their schemes of plunder. Others have withdrawn because their sectarian notions in religion were not *prevalent* here—others again, because their ambition and self-importance were not estimated according to their own ideas—others again to look after their private affairs, which they had hastily abandoned in their eagerness to enjoy advantages which they did not give themselves time to study and understand. Thus you see that the Society is gradually becoming a SELECT one, fitted to the purpose originally contemplated by its founder.

In the case of Mr. Schnee which I have cited as an example of the operation of the system, you must not imagine that he is actuated by any unworthy motives; for his devotion to the system, and high standing among us are unquestionable. He is one of the most active, intelligent, and useful members, and is perfectly happy in his present situation.

Wednesday evening.

Two of the Shakers from Kentucky arrived today to join the Society, I suspect they will not be able to find lodgings, and will therefore be obliged to return, or go somewhere else.

As Mr. S. will not agree to reduce the postage to $18\frac{3}{4}$ I have endeavored to give you 25 cents in quantity and quality. I am sure you will be satisfied with the former, whatever you may think of the latter.

Friday morning.

* * * The Baltimore Gaz. recd. yesterday evg. contains an acct. of the arrival of Mr. Owen and his son Robert Dale Owen and Capt. McDonald. They are impatiently expected here.— A great military parade yesterday afternoon and a splendid military ball in the evening at the Hall.—A great number of stran-

gers in town. Weather continues fine, though somewhat *sharp* this morning. Yr truly aff father,

Wm. Pelham.

New Harmony,
Dec. 9th, 1825.
Friday Evg. 8 o'clock.

My dear William—
   * * * The last mail brought forty six newspapers for the Gazette with 4 or 5 new applications for *exchange*. In some of them I perceive Mr. O'S [Owen's] address to "Americans" written on his passage. Mr. Wm. Owen also recd. a letter from his father dated N. York Nov. 10 in which he says he shall be here as soon as possible. By the tenor of the address, however, I suspect it will not be possible until he has spent 2 or 3 weeks at Washington City in erecting the model, and explaining his System to the Members of Congress. * * *

Your truly affectionate father,
Wm. Pelham.

December 27, 1825.
Tuesday Evening.

My Dear Son.
   * * * The weather, for several days, has been so cold and the days so short, that I could scarcely do more than make out a hasty summary for the paper, and keep myself tolerably warm— I long for the return of warm, pleasant weather. My room, now it is filled in, is a very tolerable winter room, it was pleasant enough last summer, but will be more so next season. Mr. Owen has not yet arrived, though expected daily. In the mean time many things continue unsettled, and must remain so until his return.

   For the last three weeks we have heard a great deal about a numerous assemblage of Methodists expected in this place on the 24th & 25th inst. These days are passed, but only about fifteen or twenty came, including *one* preacher. On enquiring of one of the brethern how this happened, he informed me that a report was circulated in the country that the Committee had refused them the use of the Church, though it is a notorius fact that the Committee very readily granted them the Church for the exercise of their religious worship. This is a specimen of the means resorted to, in order to injure the reputation of the Harmonians.

Facts are distorted & misrepresented, and when facts are wanting for this purpose, malevolent ingenuity can easily fabricate them. Since I became a member of this Community I have uniformly experienced every kindness that could reasonably be expected under the circumstances at present existing. No doubt there is much inconvenience, but it is in fact unavoidable, considering the hasty manner in which we have been assembled. Time, patience, and perseverance will gradually remove all difficulties. It is supposed, that on the arrival of Rob. D. Owen (now daily expected) the boarding school will be the first object of attention—that it will be reorganized under the superintendence, with the assistance of Mr. Fiquepal, Madam Fretageot & several other teachers on the Pestalozzian plan & we shall probably have Neef among us.

The routine of duty in preparing the articles for the paper is still unsettled, and will probably continue so, until Mr. Owen's arrival. At present, it is thus; Mr. [Wm.] O[wen] & Mr. J[ennings] prepare all the *editorial* articles & *decide* on the extracts to be made from the papers we receive. I make the Summary of news & submit it to their revision; the greater part of which is *accepted*, & some rejected. Mr. Palmer executes the mechanical part, pretty much in his own way. The summary of news, keeping the accounts of subscribers, and aiding Mr. P. in making up the mails seems to have fallen to my share, and, during the present season, is full as much as I want. But this department, as well as the others will undergo a full examination when Mr. O[wen] arrives, and I have every reason to believe that the management of the *library* will be committed to me, which I should be much better pleased with. It is said that Mr. O[wen] has shipped for New Orleans a large collection of books for the contemplated library.

On Sunday last, our military men as usual were paraded before the door of the Tavern, from whence they marched a little way out of town for the purpose of *drilling*, as *usual*, under the command of Mr. Jennings, who is certainly an excellent disciplinarian, & well acquainted with military tactics. This drill on *Sunday* will no doubt be called a profanation of the Sabbath, as all other Sunday Schools are, whether they be literary, or military. It is at least evident that, if a Sunday School for military instruction is a profanation, the other for clerical purposes are not less so.

Wednesday Evg.—

The regular town meeting is held this evening to hear the weekly proceedings of the Committee read, *according to custom.* I have not attended one of these meetings, or attended the Sunday lecture since the cold weather set in, for in fact I cannot risk my health so far—still, I must contrive someway or other to hear Mr. Owen when he returns. He will have some errors to correct, and many things to adjust. Among others, the affairs of the printing office, I hope I shall then have some *specific* duty assigned to me, for the present, unsettled state of things is very unpleasant to me. It seems to be the unanimous sense of the Comee. that the library shall be my destination, than which nothing cd be more agreeable to me—but as yet we have no books. Mr. Wm. O[wen] told me this evening that his father has shipped at N. York a valuable collection which will be here via New Orleans about the middle of Feb. (he thinks) but I do not expect to see them till April. I shd be glad if the books you have packed up cd be here about the same time.

Thursday Evg. Dec. 29,—6 P. M.

I have just recd. your paper of Decr. 10th with Niles Reg. of the 3rd.—This mail brot 2 letters from Wm. Blagrove, one of which contained a list of 11 subscribers he had obtained in New York. He is delighted with the System and severely regrets that his entanglements with Old Society prevents his enjoying the benefits of it—as yet—Mr. Jennings lately said that he was persuaded, if he were sent as a *Missionary* abroad, he would soon collect 30,000 persons desirous of joining the Society & really, I think he would come near the mark. I have just heard that the Yellow Spring association has "blown out." I am not surprised at this for on its commencement I anticipated a blundering business, as John Sheward will testify. When we talked of that place, I constantly said "I will go to *Head Quarters.*" Sheward will confirm this altho he cd not then coincide with me.

Mr. Owen has not yet arrived, but we have certain accounts of his being *on the road.*—You can hardly conceive the impatience with which he is expected. I just think of mentioning that we have very few *old* men—there is only one man here older than myself, Mr. Lewis, the Secretary, is about fifty, lively and active. Dr. McNamee, about the same age, Mr. Bosson abt 35, Mr. Schnee perhaps the same, Mr. Jennings I should think 30—Judge Wattles 30, Wm. Owen probably 25, but in education, experience & general knowledge not less than 35.   Still we are much in want of farmers, mechanics and laborers.

New Harmony, Ind. Jan. 6, 1826.
Friday Afternoon

My dear Son,
Yesterday evening I recd your acceptable favor of Dec. 18th with the O. Repub. of the 17th.   It seems you are puzzles about our mails,—and so am I.—Mr. Schnee told me a few days ago that letters and papers arrive sooner here when they come via Vincennes! than by any other route, altho' Vincennes appears to be abt 55 miles out of the direct way—he told me yesterday eveng that since the P. O. at Lancaster had become a distributing office the packet for Harmony is now made up *there* instead of Louisville as heretofore. * * *

Mails again.   Our Eastern mail carries all letters & papers directed to Princeton, Ind. Vincennes—Paoli—& Evansville, all along this side of the river to Albany, where it crosses to Louisville.   The E. Package contains also letters to a large portion of Kentucky as well as all places eastward.   The western mail goes to Mt. Vernon crosses the Ohio & proceeds to the Western part of Ky. a great part of Illinois, all Tennessee &c.

* * * You tell me Mr. Mills is preparing to go down the river in the spring, I shd be truly gratified to see him on his way, and I do not see any great difficulty—he can take passage in the steam boat from Cincin. to Louisville, thence to Mt. Vernon, land there & easily get a conveyance to N. Harmony—stay here as long as convenient—return to Mt. Vernon where steamboats are continually passing up & down the river as long as the water is high enough.   I pray you to present my kind remembrance to him & Mrs. Mills.

If the Society has been injured by the withdrawing of some who did not know what they were about when they joined it, the injury cannot be very extensive, for the principles supported here are daily becoming more & more known & applications for admission are still more numerous than is desirable for the Committee until better accommodations can be provided.   There is no fear of the Society being dissolved for the want of persons heartily disposed to join us—the only difficulty is house room but this I know will be removed in a great measure during the next spring, summer, & autumn.   You seem very desirous that Master Hill shd accompany you—will he be contented to lodge on the floor of my little room with you & myself? Danl Ferson will pay us a visit & I must endeavor to find some sort of lodging for him also. However, what is impracticable in this way during the cold season may not even be difficult in warm weather.

I find you have noticed "Pumpkin Vine." He is our Tavern keeper, and a queer chap he is, forever amusing himself and others with odd, biting, cutting remarks on the missionary begging scheme—the Bible & tract speculations of the clergy, &c &c &c—

I might perhaps be able to fill this sheet without fatiguing you, if I had the time, but I must hasten to a close, otherwise it cannot be sent by this mail.

Why does not Mr. Peters send us some subscribers? I am afraid he does not bestir himself as some other of our agents do. Wm. Blagrove lately sent us 12 at a slap—& promised some 20 or 30 more, all for No. 1.—No. 1 however is exhausted & therefore we were obliged to commence with No. 2.—No 7 is also out but there is some talk of reprinting both nos—and the prospectus also for a subscription paper, for which applications are made by every mail.

My dear Son—accept my tender & affectionate embrace.

Wm. Pelham.

Sunday afternoon, Jan. 8 1826.

My dear William.

On Friday last, I wrote you as long a letter as my time & engagements would permit & now I commence another in season, that I may have time to answer every point contained in yours of Decr. 11-18 which I may have overlooked.

You cannot reconcile the apparent contradiction between Mr. Owen's advertising for so many mechanics, and the Committee's rejecting applications for admission for *want of room* I will endeavor to explain it. On Mr. Owen's arrival at New York, the first news he heard of this place was that the settlement was broke up, and the members dispersed. Instead of this discouraging or disheartening him, the first thing he set about was to replenish the settlement with the population of the most useful kind, *cost what it might*. It was obvious, however, that before this could be done, the spring would be far advanced, and shifts might be made for lodging, which would be impracticable during the rigor of winter.

Monday afternoon. When I had got thus far in my letter yesterday, two of my friends called in to see me, and we sat in my little "garrett" without a fire—(the weather now being uncommonly, and unseasonably warm) conversing till nearly dark, when they left me & I repaired to Dr. McNamee's by previous invitation to supper. Here I found Mr. Lewis, Mr. Wm. Owen & a Mr. Atlee from Philadelphia, besides the Dr. & 3 or 4 ladies, besides the good lady of the house & her 2 daughters. The table was covered with a profusion of delicacies, excellent coffee, tea, cream, honey, sweetmeats, ham, sausage, &c &c in abundance— But I would not have you infer that this good cheer is found in every family in New Harmony,—the time has not yet arrived when *all the members* are to fare alike—though I really believe this will be the case in the *new Community*. In the meantime, contentment sweetens the cup of life, whatever it may contain. Now do not run to the other extreme, and imagine we are starved for this is not true, tho our privations are sometimes such as to test the strength of our principles. * * *

After the enjoyment of a pleasant evening I came home about 9 o'clock & soon after went to bed.

I never see the Philadelphia Gaz. but from a humorous extract which will appear in our next gazette, I should judge that it was not decidedly hostile. The Sat. Ev. Post comes regularly to us, According to your suggestion, I shall offer an exchange to the Western Carrier, Ravenna, O. * * *

You make me laugh when you talk about "Pone Bread, & Musquetoes." The good book saith, "better is a crust of bread with contentment of mind, than the most sumptous fare where there is no love." I know I have not quoted exactly, but I have no bible at hand. Apropos; Do not forget to send me our family 4to bible. Pone Bread & Musquetoes! How wonderfully efficient these will be in defeating the most feasible plan for improving the condition of mankind that was ever devised.

Mr. Hill seems uncertain whether he will visit us or not. I hope you are not so, for I shall be truly disappointed, & grieved if you do not come. This expectation has a considerable share in keeping up my spirit—another source of comfort to me has been the uniform kindness of your expressions and the *cheerful tone* of your letters. * * *

On looking over the list of articles (Nov. 7) packed up in the trunk, I perceive "Book for Map of the World— & U. S." I hope you will contrive to send me the large maps to which they refer.— I see also that [you] have already packed up the Family Bible. The map belonging to Lewis & Clark is in a red leather 8to book cover somewhere about the book shelves.—I had scarcely written the last word "shelves" when Mr. Palmer's young man brot me a proof of the outside of our next paper (i. e.—pages 1st, 4, 5 & 8th.) to be corrected. It contains some excellent matter—especially the "Gray Light No. 4" on the *"Origin of evil;"* a subject which has always puzzled the wisest heads in the world. There is likewise a good letter signed "A Christian." I know not who is the writer of the letter, tho' I might know if I thought it worth the trouble of enquiring. The Grey Light is a communication from N. York by mail—I wish you would occasionally make extracts from our Gazette & especially the 2 Nos. of the "Grey Light." * * *

I am at present, as I have been, a boarder (now at 64 cents a week) with my *old friends* the *young* baker, 22 years of age, & his *young* wife, about 20, where I am as comfortably situated with regard to diet as cd reasonably be expected. Their house is situated on the main street, about 200 yards from my lodging. We have no occasion to be governed by the ringing of the bell for meals, but I find it convenient for us all to take our breakfast at 8—our dinner at ½ past 12 & our supper at dark. They have been uniformly kind, & attentive to my convenience, & I believe we are mutually pleased with each other. * * *

We have heard nothing yet from Mr. O[wen]—the word however now is, that the river havg risen considerably we shall hear his voice in the *Steeple house* next Sunday.

The weather continues so warm that I have taken off *two* blankets from my bed. You may tell Mr. Harris that the Doctor's sick list contains about 20 names—and he will observe that is a much greater number than ever were sick at the same time in *Zanesville* or any where else except Harmony.—The force of prejudice is astonishing to those who have never attended to its effect on *mental vision*. I have lately recd. from Neef a curious letter on this subject.—

Wednesday morng. The weather continues uncommonly warm, we have scarcely seen the face of the Sun for the last 6 or 7 days,—the thermometer on Monday morn stood at 61— and judging by my feelings it is about the same now. A good deal of rain has fallen—but the ground is now dry tho' the sky continues cloudy?—If this warm weather continues much longer we may expect to hear some *musqueto* music.

Wed. evg.—The weather has changed, and we have again enjoyed the splendid light of the sun—the evening is clear & the sky again presents a brilliant assemblage of stars. This is the evening on which our town meetings are weekly held, but they ceased to *interest me as soon as the cold weather commenced*. I prefer sitting here in my comfortable little room, and scribbling what may, or perhaps may not interest you. *The report today* was that Mr. Owen was *actually seen* yesterday at Mt. Vernon with a company of 32 persons on their way to Harmony. "A plague on all liars" say I—for if this had been true he would have been here by noon this day. * * *

Upon looking over my pass-book just now I find a balance of $24.29 in my favor.—From this must be deducted the charge against me for washing, at the rate of 16 cents a doz. and for postage, since my franking privilege ceased.

Thursday noon. The weather has again become sharp, cold and clear, and the glorious sun shines out most brilliantly—No news of Mr. O[wen] yet.

Friday morng. Cloudy again with rain & thunder!—I have the pleasure of saying that Mr. O[wen] *is here*—he arrived yesterday evg. accompanied only by a Russian lady whom he accidently found somewhere below Stubenville on her way to New Harmony. An assembly of almost the whole population met in the *Steeple house* about 7 o'clock—Mr. O[wen] entered & taking his stand in the pulpit expressed the pleasure and joy he felt to be among us. I have not time to give you a sketch of his discourse which he soon closed. He earnestly recommended Unity & brotherly love. He said that he had left his company behind proceeding in a boat which contained more *learning* than ever was before contained in a boat. He did not mean Latin & Greek & other languages but real substantial knowledge. It contained some of the ablest instructors of youth that cd be found in the U. S. or perhaps in the world. I was pleased with his manner as well as his matter. I have not yet been introduced to him, preferring to wait till the *bustle* is over. He is to give a lecture next Sunday in the forenoon. In noticing his passing through Z. you do not say (in the O. Republic) that he gave a lecture. I hope, however, you saw and spoke to him.

     Your truly affectionate father,
          Wm. Pelham.

     N. Harmony, Friday Jan. 27, 1826.
My dear Son,

 Yesterday evening I recd your acceptable letter of Jan. 8 with 2 Ravenna Papers but no O. Repub. *At the same time* I recd. your long looked for letter of the 31st Oct!! which appears to have been missent to Peoria Ill. and forwarded from thence on the 12th inst. * * *

When I commenced writing this I intended, if possible to fill the sheet but I now begin to suspect it will not be in my power, for I have at this moment 4 visotors in my room, talking to me and to one another about the *New Constitution* which is about to be formed. As soon as this is accomplished this preliminary Society will be dissolved and we shall immediately commence a *Cummunity of Equality* & mutual cooperation. I would willingly give you some account of the proceedings which have already taken place with this view. Since his return Mr. Owen has delivered frequent lectures, and yesterday evening a committee of 7 was chosen by ballot to draw up a Constitution and a set of Rules & Regulations to be submitted to the Members of the present Society, article by article. Some of my friends thought proper to run me for this committee, and I received 44 purely *unsolicited* votes—the highest number for any person was 136—(Mr. Owen himself)— and the lowest *successful* number of votes was 63. In fact I did not know (& cared not at all)— that my name was thought of, till yesterday about noon & I assure you I speak sincerely in saying that I am *glad* that the number of votes in favor of electing me did not reach the point of election. I was by no means desirous of being placed in the Committee. As soon as things are settled I will write you an acct. of them, unless I shall have the supreme satisfaction of seeing you here. Since the rect. of your letters I have had no time to read them attentively, & my chief purpose in writing this is to inform you of their coming to hand.

Wednesday night 10 o'clock.

Since the date of the above I have been so constantly occupied that I have had no opportunity of continuing my *journal* for your information. Besides the weather has been so cold, that a great part of my time has been consumed in protecting myself against its effects. This day however, it has moderated *considerably* & I am now sitting in my room scribbling what I think may be interesting to you.

This evening was appointed to report the draft of the *Constitution* prepared by the Committee appointed for that purpose. It is in print & I shall enclose a copy in the Gazette directed to the Ohio Repub. But you are to consider it as a proposal only not yet acted upon by the Society. A plan of **Arrangement of** the affairs of the Society was also presented to the meeting and ordered to be printed. If this be done in time I will also enclose that. The more I see of Mr. Owen the more I am convinced of his prudence, wisdom, integrity and enlarged benevolence. The purity of his views is *unquestionable*, whatever may be said by the enemies of the New Social System. Every article of this Constitution is to undergo a thorough investigation in a public assembly of the Society when the utmost freedom of speech is not only *tolerated* but solicited and encouraged. Young and old are equally invited to express their sentiments, and the common sense & common feeling of the Society decide on their propriety. This is a delightful state of society, and such as I have long entertained in *idea*, but never expected to see *realized*. It will yet be some time, perhaps a week or two before the Society will be able *finally* to determine on their constitution & code of laws.

The persons who have lately arrived are Mr. Wm. Maclure of Philad. reputed to be immensely rich, and certainly *devoted* to the principles of this Society. I have had several interviews and conversations with him and his manners and sentiments are in direct opposition to those of all other *wealthy* men of whom I have any knowledge, excepting only Mr. Owen himself. Besides him we have Mr. Fiquepal & Madam Fretageot, both Pezzalozzian teachers,—Mr. LeSueur an eminent designer, Mr. Say, Dr. Troost, a distinguished mineralogist—and several other men of Science. Mr. MaClure has put into my hands a catalogue of French books and philosophical apparatus now at New Orleans on their way to this place amounting in value to 100,000 francs and weighing abt 50 tons. He wished me to make a fair transcript of the invoice in a book he had provided for the purpose. I shall find some difficulty in doing this for want of a good French dictionary—but I will accomplish it.

Thursday Forenoon.

By the last mail I recd. a letter from Neef,—he is anxious to be among us, but cannot yet bring matters to bear—Mr. MaClure told me yesterday that he wrote to him by the last mail, urging him to come on immediately whether he brings his family and movable property or not, and in the latter case to make arrangements for their following him, for that he was already a Member. This letter of Mr. MaClure's I expect will settle his mind, and we shall probably see him in a week or two.

The plan of the proposed Constitution is in the hands of all the members, and will undergo a thorough investigation. My mind during the last two weeks has been in a state of such constant excitement, as to be painful, and this you will easily conceive when you consider how inactive both in mind and body I have long been previous to my coming hither. I feel now that I want quietness and rest, and I scarcely expect any, until I am appointed *Librarian* which will in all probability be my permanent occupation. Mr. Owen and all the members of the Committee, besides a considerable part of the population appear to think me most fitted for such employment, and it exactly squares with my own inclination.

The bell is now ringing for dinner, immediately after which I must go the Printing Office & assist Mr. Palmer in making up at least 300 papers to be sent by mail. If I have the oppy. of making any addition to this letter I will embrace it, but I rather think it will not be in my power. The warm weather will soon return & I anxiously hope it will bring you along.—

Thursday night. I have just inclosed in a wrapper seperate from the usual inclosure which Mr. Palmer directed to the "Ohio Repub. Zanesville, O." a duplicate No. 19 of the Gazette with the proposed Constitution & Plan of Arrangement.

These are busy times. Meetings are held almost every night in the *Steeple House;* and at the farthest every second night the bell is rung at ½ past 6 and at 7 no vacant seat can be found.— I have hitherto attended them all— but this evening I shall *take my rest*, as I expect the business will chiefly be some verbal criticisms on the Constitution and proposals to amend the phraseology—Everyone gives his sentiments freely, and it is really remarkable that so little uninteresting matter is brought forward. Some of our mechanics are truly eloquent, and none absurd. It would be no amusement to you if I were to give you my crude remarks on the proposed constitution, for I have not had time to read it attentively,—but I certainly do anticipate some considerable alterations in the style of it.—Several other drafts will be offered to the consideration of the Society and which of them will ultimately be preferred, it is impossible at present to say.

It is now between 8 & 9 & I shall go directly to bed—so, good night, my dear boy, & let me still cherish the hope of seeing you here when the season is favorable.

Wednesday Feb. 8", 1826.

My dear Son,

The Constitution, of which I sent you a printed sketch, has

undergone a thorough examination and discussion; and was recommitted to the Constitutional Committee who again reported it, with considerable alterations and amendments. After these were fully discussed, and some further amendments made the Society finally adopted a Constitution, which would have appeared in this day's paper, if it could have been prepared in season. There being no printed copy, I cannot present you with the articles. It has been transcribed into a book, and 300 names have already been subscribed to it. There will be very few, if any dissentients among the members of the Preliminary Society.

This evening is appointed for the election of three important officers, viz. Secretary, Treasurer & Commissary, and it is expected that the organization of the Community will be completed next week. Every department will be arranged so as to produce a united effort to furnish every practicable means of comfortable subsistence to every individual. Hitherto, there has been much irregularity of effort, the consequence of which nearly paralyzed the energies of the population, but at length I see the way clear, and I see the utter impossibility of such a state of things again recurring. The several parts of the *great machine* will be so admirably adapted to each other, as to effect the most valuable purposes. The experience I have gained convinces me I was right in coming here, in preference to going to any of the *Communities* professedly formed on Mr. Owen's principles in other parts of the country. During the last 8 months the want of organization and arrangement has caused much perplexity and difficulty, and the introduction now of order and regularity into the several departments will be comparatively easy. I anticipate that in 6 months the New Harmony machine will go like a piece of clock work. The preceeding errors are noted and will be avoided. In consequence of the great change which has been just made, I should not be surprised to see it announced in some of the Eastern papers, with *great glee* that Mr. Owen's visionary project on the banks of the Wabash has utterly failed, &c &c. tho nothing can be further from the truth—for in reality one third of it is accomplished— and we are just entering on the second 3d and the next step—(when we are prepared for it) will be into the Village of Equality and Independence. He is an extraordinary man— a wonderful man—such a one indeed as the world has never before seen. His wisdom, his comprehensive mind, his practical knowledge, but above all, his openness, candor & sincerity, have no parallel in ancient or modern history. Do not think I am dreaming, for in fact, I have closely attended to his language and movements since his return.

I earnestly expect to see you here early in the spring when you will have opportunity of seeing, of hearing & judging for yourself. There is now here a young married man from a distant part of this State. He came about a month ago and has resided at the Tavern at the expense of 3 dollars a week for himself and his horse. He has felt so deeply interested in the measures preparatory to the formation of the New Community that he could quit us until he saw its accomplishment. We have spent a good deal of time together & I expect he will shortly set out on his return for the purpose of bringing his wife & child & 4 other families who will accompany him, if he can obtain a previous assurance that they will be received.

Thursday afternoon.—The election was not held yesterday evening, as I had expected it would be. It will probably take place this evening. It is generally thought that Mr. Lewis will be *Secretary*, and Wm. Owen *Treasurer*, the Commissary is rather more doubtful.

There is—Thursday night—I have been to the P. O. and got the O. Repub. of Jany. 21, with letters from Col. Chambers, Mr. Harris and Mr. Neef & none from yourself. There seems to be a great improvement in the expedition of the mail. Col. C's letter is dated Jan. 22d & Mr. Harris' is dated 24th. Tho after all it seems to require 12 or 14 days to come fr. Z. to H. Neef's letter bears the postmark of Louisville Jan. 30". By the bye, do not omit to call at the P. O. in Louisville on your way hither. You will *probably* find a letter there tho I am not certain. If you can contrive to see Mr. Neef he would be most happy to meet with you. He has a daughter in Louisville whom you may find by enquiring of my friend Mr. Taylor, the Post Office Clerk. Tell Col. Chambers I will not fail to answer all his inquiries as soon as possible, but he must not be impatient, for these are *busy times* for every one in New Harmony. If he will have patience till *warm weather* I shall better be able to satisfy him. The proceedings of the Convention in forming the *Community Constitution* with the Constitution itself will be in the next paper and I will send him a copy. I think I informed you, and I wish you would mention to Col. Chambers & Mr. Harris that soon after Mr. Owen's return he was followed by his son Robert Dale Owen, Dr. Price & Mr. Wm. MaClure of Philadelphia, Mr. Whitwell, Mr. LeSueur, Mr. Say, all men of extensive scientific knowledge,

Mr. Fiquepal and Madam Fretageot first rate teachers on the Pestalozzian plan. There are now at New Orleans on their way hither a vast collection of books, philosophical apparatus & musical instruments weighing upwards of 50 tons & the freight of which will cost 10 to 1200 dollars. In Harmony there will be the best Library & the best School in the United States.

10 O'clock P. M.—The election is again postponed till tomorrow evening, to give further time for the members to form their judgment. My own, indeed, is already formed, and I earnestly hope the election may fall on Mr. Lewis, Wm. Owen, and Richardson Whitby, who came here from a society of shakers in Kentucky, and brought with him a practical knowledge of the order and regularity, and system, by which that society has distinguished itself. This is an anxious time,—(not with a view to a *final* success and of our principles, which must infalliably succeed sooner or later) but with a view to the *speedy* accomplishment of the purposes for which we are associated. It is therefore important that our first selection of agents be made with the greatest circumspection, and due appreciation of the qualifications of the persons choosen to carry into effect the principles which we advocate and support. Forseeing that I shall have no opportunity of continuing this letter tomorrow, and unwilling to send you any *blank* paper, I may as well endeavor to fill the remainder of my sheet with such matters as occur to me now.

You will easily conceive the effect produced on the minds of our citizens when Mr. Owen, after some days examination of the State of things here, proposed the immediate formation of a Community of Equality and mutual cooperation. The subject was debated with the utmost freedom, which he encouraged by constant efforts to make every one speak his *real* sentiments wheather favorable or unfavorable to his proposal. After a full and *verily*, a *free* discussion the proposal was accepted, and we have since been constantly engaged in devising the means by which it can be effected. Next week after your receiving this you will see the constitution and plan of arrangement, and you will perceive that every feature bears the stamp of *genuine* democracy, not the false democracy of the office seekers of Zanesville.

$\frac{1}{2}$ past ten. Mr. Bosson has just come in and brought me Mr. Peters' kind & affectionate letter of Jan. 16th. * * * Goodnight, Dr William. Wm. Pelham.

Feb. 23, 1826.—Friday.

My Dear William—

I have snatched up the first sheet of paper I could lay my hands on (for want of time to seek a better one) to acknowledge the receipt of yours of Feb. 5—7, postmarked Feb. 7 which came to hand yesterday evening. I cannot at present enter into particulars, but I have enquired about the Steamboat charges. The result is that from Cincinnati to Louisville the charge is probably 4 dollars & from Louisville to Mt. Vernon 8 dollars—perhaps something less.

Our affairs still remain in an unsettled state, the consequence of which is much inconvenience in a variety of ways. There is more to be done at once than can be to place things on the right footing. Three days ago Mr. Owen informed me that Mr. Jennings had declined the editorship of the paper any longer, and he, (Mr. Owen) wished me to undertake it. I answered him that I considered that duty a very important one, and I did not conceive myself by any means adequate to the task. He said that I should have assistance when I required it. But I know full well the difference between promising & performing, however as he seemed to expect it of me, I prepared the 2 editorial articles in the last Gazette, and shewed them to him, before they were inserted.

Your suggestion concerning a direct rout to Indianapolis, is well worthy of attention. It shall be communicated to Mr. Owen, and measures, shall, if possible be put in train to effect the object in view. * * *

I have not time to write more, but will endeavor to send you another letter next week.

Your truly affectionate Father,

Wm. Pelham.

I have had a smart touch of the prevailing Influenza but am now recovering—it has pulled me down considerably.—My face is thin and pale—I believe I have lost 10 pounds of flesh within the last 4 or 5 weeks—but I expect the approach of warm weather will restore me.

Thursday Afternoon, Mar. 16", 1826.

My dear William.

I have just finished helping Mr. Palmer, (according to custom) to make up our mails and I have a few minutes left before I shall be called upon to open the mail, Mr. Schnee being absent. About 3 or 4 weeks ago Mr. Owen accosted me with a *wish* that I would undertake to conduct the Gazette as Mr. Jennings had declined it on *account of his health*. I answered that I considered it an important concern, and that I was not competent to the task. To make a long story short, he urged it and I merely acquiested. In this new capacity I have done as well as I could, though not so well as I wished. How long this will continue to be my occupation is uncertain. Dr. Buchanan of Shelbyville, Ky. has *at last* been written to, to be the editor, but our hopes of his coming are very slim. I shall be heartily glad to get rid of this burden as soon as possible.

Since I last wrote to you very considerable changes have taken place in our affairs, and the prospect is now daily improving. Mr. Owen is indefatigable in his endeavors to introduce economy, frugality, industry, equality, and other practices essential to the success of his principles. In the meantime I do not doubt you very frequently hear the most unfavorable accounts of this place; but you need not fear a dissolution of this Society, for *it cannot happen*. Various modifications have been, and probably will be made, without touching the foundation, which stands on a rock, not to be shaken by priestcraft or any other worldly craft.

You will perceive that I have given a new complexion to the Gaz. in discouraging those long-winded metaphysical disquisitions with which Mr. J. was wont to fill its columns. There are some able pens employed in the service of the Gaz. and when we *get in order* I am in hopes the paper will become more useful than it has hitherto heen. You will understand that my criticisms on the paper are entirely confidential. I just hear the Mail Stage horn at a distance.

Friday Afternoon.—*Miscellany*. The mail yesterday was unusually small. I recd. neither a letter nor an Ohio Repub. I shall anxiously look for you during the whole of next month. I would wish you to *deposite in your memory* all you hear of us either *good* or *bad*, though I am aware your mind will not be overlooked with reports of the former description. It might not be amiss to make notes, to assist yr memory. The fare from Cincinn to Louisville is about 4 dollars, from L. to Mt. Vernon about 6. Mr. Neef is expected to be here this evening or tomorrow.

I would willing communicate with you further, if I did not feel too cold & uncomfortable & moreover had a convenient situation for writing. I should like you to come alone if you do not accompany Daniel Ferson.

Farewell my dear Son—Let me have the supreme satisfaction

of seeing you in April at furthest. In the meantime present me most kindly to Mr. Peters & Mary and all other friends.

Wm. Pelham.

The following letter from Wm. Creese Pelham written a few weeks before his Father's death, gives some information in connection with the schools and Educational Society of New Harmony.

New Harmony, Wednesday 10 January 1827.

My Dear Father

I was unavoidably detained in school longer this evening than I wished and cannot write you as much as I wished. Bolton and myself have several times agreed to come out to you but have been detained by "counteracting circumstances" such as rainy days and cold days &c but we shall be with you next Sunday or the Sunday following I think.—

We go on in the same old way, changing every thing, somethimes before we have an opportunity to find out its benefits. In the internal arrangements of our society no very considerable changes have been made. Dunn & Johnson have left us. We have received between 30 & 40 children from Mr. Owen's Community as day scholars at No. 2. Mr. McCall has a class and Mr. Brown, they come as day scholars at eight dollars per year. All the other children attend at Madam's at No. 5, where some are well satisfied with their progress and others the contrary as usual. Dr. Embree, a young man from Cincinnati delivers lectures to them on physiology and dissects pigs and dogs &c for their information.

Phiquepal has taken his boys entirely to himself and lives in the Church and hall. Jones and his wife are part of his community and Simms &c. The Carpenters, Shoemakers and all persons not employed in teaching the children have removed from the Church. Thirwell has taken all his tools &c home. Phiquepal has stopped his boys from making shoes for the community, which created some dissatisfaction.

A resolution was passed a short time since by our society forbiding the use of the Hall for dancing &c, without special permission of the society. This week, on the application of Miss Caroline Tiebout, one of our members, a resolution was passed for a ball this evening, but on the earnest representation of Phiquepal that it was impossible to use the Hall for dancing without interfering with his arrangements, the resolution was repealed, and we need expect no more balls in the Hall unless they be on Sunday afternoon as proposed by Mr. Owen, but which meets with great opposition.

Phiquepal's boys sleep in the rooms formerly Lesueur and Troost's in the Hall and go to bed at eight and rise at four when they receive one of their lessons, a lecture I believe from Phiquepal. He has his school room which is likewise his eating room &c covered with skeletons, bones, arithmometers &c &c so that it looks more like a museum than a schoolroom.

The prospect of our leaving here in the spring brightens. I earnestly hope we may not be disappointed. Dr. Price writes from Cincinnati that Neville can be purchased of Gen. Neville with 2600 acres of excellent land for $15000. The Gen. wishes to become a member of the community. A part of the property which is rented produced to the Gen. on an average of 35 bush. of corn per acre being one third of the actual produce. A new steam engine which cost $2600 was put in the mill last year. (a saw and grist mill) there are several good brick houses &c &c. The improvements put on the place by Piate cost $24000, since which Gen. Neville has expended several thousand,—but all this is not talked of publicly yet,—a meeting was held at Thirwell's last evening on the subject and mem. furnished Lees who is going up the river shortly. Dr. Price writes he has no doubt but the money can be raised at any time in Cincinnati and considered as a speculation it is the greatest one ever offered and nothing but the General being such a devoted community man could ever induce him to make the offer &c.

I believe our Rope factory burned down before you were here last, and No. 4 was on fire yesterday but little damage was done. Our Society is still tearing down the log buildings for firewood, and the women sometimes cannot agree among themselves who is the cook. Burton and Beal were the cooks at the Granary last week. The dining tables have all been removed from the Granary into the sitting room at the Green House. Three tables accomodate all who eat there. The reason for this was that the Granary was cold and Phiquepal having taken his boys &c away left but few who might be more comfortably accomodated in the sitting room—the room East of that now used for our meetings. Tiebout has resigned his office of storekeeper.

Our Scientific Journal has not yet been commenced but the plates for it are engraving and preparations making. The Printing press &c have been removed to the Infirmary or old carpenter shop.

Say was married the other day to Lucy Sistare, they went off to a place beyond Springfield. * * *

Your aff. Son

Wm. Creese Pelham.

A letter from William Owen to William Pelham of Zanesville, O.

Harmonie, Indiana
22—January 1825

Sir—

In my Father's absence I have received your letters dated the 1—& 24—of last month.

My father sailed up the river from Mount Vernon about 10 days ago, in company with Mr. Rapp and 70 or 80 Harmonians who were on their way to Economy, a property lately purchased by them near Pittsburg. My Father intends proceeding to the City of Washington without delay, hoping to come into communication there, with most of the leading minds in the States. As soon as he has made known, as far as he considers necessary, the leading features of his plans, he will then return to this place as quickly as possible, in order to complete the arrangements necessary to the formation of a Society here, founded on the Principles, which he has so long advocated; for which purpose he purchased this estate from Mr. Rapp, a few days before his departure.

I am highly gratified to learn that you have been pleased by the perusal of the Dublin Journal, containing an account of my Fathers proceedings while in that City.

At present we have no further publication here; but we are in expectation of receiving several shortly from Europe. When they arrive I am sure my Father will have much pleasure in giving you every information on the subject.

As it is intended to form an establishment here with the least possible loss of time, I fear my Father will be prevented from seeing you at Zanesville, before his return to this town; but I am sure he will take the earliest opportunity of cultivating a personal acquaintance with you.

It is proposed that a Society be formed here, on the Principle of united production and consumption, to be composed of persons practicing all the most useful occupations necessary to the well being of a complete establishment, to whom lodgings, food clothing, attendance during sickness and a good education for their children will be secured. The profits to accumulate in order to form a new Community on the Principle of complete equality, as soon as a sufficient sum shall be realized. In case of expulsion or Voluntary Departure each family to be entitled to draw out all the property they may have brought in with them, and to receive in addition whatever the Directors of the establishment may consider reasonable.

We expect a number of useful tradesmen to come out from Europe in November or December and that we shall be joined by many others both from the Eastern States and from this neighborhood.

I shall forward your letter to Washington City by tomorrow's post. My Father, I think, will be with us again early in March. We shall be happy to see you here whenever you cam make it convenient to leave home and I have no doubt, my Father will endeavor to make his arrangements to visit you if possible, on his return Westward.

With best thanks for your good wishes, believe me
Your Obt. Servt.
Wm. Owen.

PART TWO

From *Travels through North America, during the year 1825 and 1826*, by His Highness, Bernhard, Duke of Saxe-Weimer Eisenach [1828], Vol. II., pp. 105-124.

BERNHARD, KARL, *Duke of Saxe-Weimer.*

Duke Bernhard tells us that the idea of visiting America occupied his mind almost from the earliest years, the chief reason being "I wished to see the new world; the country; the people; their conditions and institutions; their customs and manners." But due to the exactions of the military life, this desire was not granted until rather late in years. Finally in 1825 the opportunity came, and due to the friendship that existed between himself and the king of the Netherlands, the latter provided passage for him on a royal sloop of war—The Pallas.

Duke Bernhard spent fifteen months in this country. By training he was a keen observer, and his accounts therefore are of more than usual interest.

The Wabash, a very beautiful river, rises not far from the sources of the Miami of the Lakes, and meanders through one of the most fertile districts of the west. At its mouth, it is about two hundred and fifty yards broad, and is navigable about four hundred miles. The Wabash forms the boundary between the states of Illinois and Indiana, the right bank belongs to the former, the left to the latter state. About evening, the steamboat landed Mr. Huygens and myself on the right bank at Mount Vernon, a place established about two years ago, whence we proposed to go by land to New Harmony. Mr. Hottinguer left us, as he pursued his voyage in the steam-boat; I parted very reluctantly from this esteemed fellow traveller, who possessed many good qualities, above all others, one seldom found in his countrymen, great modesty.

Mount Vernon lies upon a high bank, one hundred and twenty-six miles from New Orleans, and eight hundred and three from Pittsburgh. It is a favourable situation for trade, laid out on an extensive plan, but has only frame houses, and at most three hundred inhabitants. It is the new capital of Posey county. A prison was finished for the use of the county; a court-house was about to be built. We formed an acquaintance with a physician established here, and a travelling merchant. The roots of the felled trees remained yet in the streets of the town, the woods began close behind the houses; nay, the latest built were encircled by them.

On the following morning, 15th of April, we hired a two-horse wagon, to carry us to the village of New Harmony, which is sixteen miles distant from Mount Vernon, and lies on the left shore of the Wabash. The road passed through a hilly country, thickly grown with green-leaved trees. The way was made very bad by former rains, and the most miry places were mended with logs, forming a grievous causeway;* over a little stream, called Big creek, we crossed a tolerable wooden bridge. About half way is Springfield, at first made the capital of Posey county, which, however, afterwards was changed to Mount Vernon, as I have mentioned before. In Springfield the county gaol still remains, also a brick court-house, and about ten wooden houses, two of them are taverns. As the road was very bad, and the horses went very slow, I walked at least ten miles, and arrived at New Harmony, before the carriage. As soon as you clear the woods, you have a very handsome view of the place. It lies in a valley, not far from the Wabash. The woody and low banks of this river, were at present, in the neighbourhood of New Harmony, overflowed. From the roots of trees still remaining, it was visible, that this country had been covered with wood but a short time back.

In fact, it is but eleven years since Mr. Rapp with his society, after they had disposed of Harmony in Pennsylvania, moved here, and felled the first tree to found New Harmony in a country inhabited only by wolves, Indians, bears, rattlesnakes, &c.

The hills immediately next to the place, are already cleared of timber of the larger kind; they are converted into vineyards, and partly into orchards. Farther off are meadows and fields to the right, and to the left fruit and vegetable gardens, carefully enclosed by palisades. New Harmony itself, has broad unpaved streets, in which good brick houses appear alternately, with framed cabins and log houses: the streets are regular, running at right angles. We took up our quarters in the only tavern there, belonging to the community; it was passable.

Rapp's society, called from their former residence, the Harmonites, consisted of Wurtemburgers. Their early history is known, and perhaps, when I visit this society from Pittsburgh in their new establishment, "Economy," I may find an opportunity

*["These log turnpikes are better known by the name of "corduroy roads."]
TRANS.

to say more concerning them. Rapp sold New Harmony in the year, 1825, to the Englishman, Robert Owen, and left there with his people on the 5th of May, to go up the Ohio to Economy. Mr. Owen was originally engaged in manufactures, and possessed a large cotton factory at New Lanark, on the Falls of Clyde, ten miles from Glasgow in Scotland, where he had, by the adoption of a new system of education and formation of character, changed a collection of one thousand rude labourers into a community of industrious beings. His system, and his ideas upon the situation of human society, as well as the improvements that are capable of being made, he has divulged in a series of essays, which are collected, and appear in print under the name of a new view of society. They conclude with the project of a constitution for a community formed on his system.

Mr. Owen is an enemy to all sects, the spirit of which has generated so much evil under the imposing name of religion. He allows each person liberty to believe in what he may consider to be good; so that a pure Deism is the peculiar religion of his adherents. On this account he was very obnoxious to the prevailing sects in Great Britain, and accordingly his system could not extend itself there. He was therefore induced to turn this attention to the United States, and particularly to the western part of the Union, where, as he says, there is less hypocrisy of religion prevailing than to the east. He then purchased New Harmony from Mr. Rapp, and commenced his establishment in the month of May last. As he laid the foundation of it entirely on perfect equality and community of property, many enthusiasts in these principles from various parts of the Union joined themselves to him; and also a number of vagabonds and lazy worthless persons, from all parts of the worlds, that would willingly live well at the public expense, who had drank away the little money, if they brought any at all, at the tavern, and who would not work, but desired to say a great deal. Mr. Owen had gone to England on account of business in the month of July, and during his absence, a complete anarchy had been introduced into the new community. At the end of October he arrived from England at New York on his return, gave lectures there, in Philadelphia, and in Washington, upon his system, made some proselytes in Philadelphia, and came back to New Harmony. He lamented over his people, and brought the situation of anarchy in which they had fallen before their eyes so plainly, with the consequences resulting therefrom, that they invested him with dictatorial authority for one year.

In the eastern states there is a general dislike to him. It was thought unadvised that he issued a proclamation to the Americans on his last arrival in New York, in which he told them, that among many virtues they possessed great faults, among which he alluded to an ill-directed propensity to religious feelings, and proposed himself as their reformer in this respect. I heard at that time unfavourable expressions from persons in the highest public offices against him; and one of them gave Mr. Owen to understand very plainly that he considered his intellects rather deranged.* In one family alone, where theory took place of experimental knowledge, did I hear conversation turn to his advantage.

After all this, I came with the utmost expectation to New Harmony, curious to become acquainted with a man of such extraordinary sentiments. In the tavern, I accosted a man very plainly dressed, about fifty years of age, rather of low stature, who entered into a conversation with me, concerning the situation of the place, and the disordered state in which I would find every thing, where all was newly established, &c. When I asked this man how long before Mr. Owen would be there, he announced himself, to my no small surprize, as Mr. Owen, was glad at my visit, and offered himself to show every thing, and explain to me whatever remained without explanation. As the arrangement calculated for Rapp's society was not adapted to his, of course many alterations would naturally be made. All the log houses still standing in the place, he intended to remove, and only brick and framed edifices should be permitted to remain. Also all enclosures about particular gardens, as well as all the enclosures within the place itself, he would take away, and only allow the public highways leading through the settlement to be enclosed. The whole should bear a resemblance to a park, in which the separate houses should be scattered about.

In the first place, Mr. Owen carried me to the quondam church of Rapp's society; a simple wooden building, with a steeple of the same materials, provided with a clock. This church was at present appropriated to joiner's and shoemaker's shops, in which the boys are instructed in these mechanic arts.

Behind the church stands a large brick edifice, built in the form of a cross, and furnished with a species of cupola, the purpose

*[This is perhaps, the most charitable idea that can be formed of the actions of such reformers, as well as of a "lady heretofore mentioned, who has unsexed herself, and become so intoxicated with vanity, as enthusiastically to preach up a "reformation" in favour of the promiscuous intercourse of sexes and colours, the downfall of all religion, and the removal of all restraints imposed by virtue and morality!]—TRANS.

of which is unknown. Rapp, they say, had dreamed three times that this building should be erected, and therefore he had it done; but it is thought, and I believe correctly, that he only did this to keep his society in constant employment, so that they could have no leisure to reflect upon their situation, and dependence upon him. His power over them actually extended so far, that to prevent his society from too great an increase, he forbid the husbands from associating with their wives. I also heard here a report which I had already been apprised of in Germany, that he had himself castrated a son who had transgressed this law, for the sake of an example, and that the son had died under the operation. Over one of the entrances of this problematical edifice, stands the date of the year 1822, hewed in stone; under it is a gilt rose, and under this is placed the inscription Micah. 4 v. 8. The interior of the house forms a large hall, in form of a cross, the ceiling is supported by wooden pillars. Mr. Owen has devoted the hall to the purposes of dancing, music, and meetings for philosophical discussions. He told me that he intended to have the ends of the cross, both of the grand saloon as well as those of the hall under the roof, divided off by partitions, so as to use them for school-rooms, for a library, for a cabinet of natural history, of physical objects, &c.

Mr. Owen then conducted me to Rapp's former dwelling, a large, well-built brick house, with two lightning rods. The man of God, it appeared, took especial good care of himself; his house was by far the best in the place, surrounded by a garden with a flight of stone steps, and the only one furnished with lightning rods. Mr. Owen, on the contrary, contented himself with a small apartment in the same tavern where I lodged. At present, the offices, and the residence of Mr. M'Clure, the associate of Mr. Owen, are in Rapp's house.*

Mr. M'Clure is a man distinguished for learning, who has published a geological chart of the United States. He told me that he was in Germany in the year 1802, and also at Weimar, where he had become acquainted with the literati residing there. I was introduced by him to a native of Alsace, of the name of Neef, a rather aged man, who had the superintendence of the boys. Mr. Owen's two eldest sons were also here shown to me, pupils of Fellenberg, who is greatly respected. Afterwards Mr. Owen made me acquainted with Mr. Lewis, secretary of the society

*[It is understood that Mr. M'Clure has long since given up all connexion with the New Harmony bubble.]—TRANS.

from Virginia, and a relation of the great Washington. He was already pretty far advanced in years, and appeared to have united himself to the society from liberal principles, as far as I could judge from our short conversation. Another acquaintance that I made, was with a Mr. Jennings, from Philadelphia, a young man, who was educated as a clergyman, but had quitted that profession to follow this course of life, and had united himself to Mr. Owen. He intended, nevertheless, to leave this place again, and return back to Philadelphia. Many other members have the same design, and I can hardly believe that this society will have a long duration.* Enthusiasm, which abandons its subjects but too soon, as well as the itch for novelty, had contributed much to the formation of this society. In spite of the principles of equality which they recognize, it shocks the feelings of people of education, to live on the same footing with every one indiscriminately, and eat with them at the same table.

The society consisted, as I was informed, of about one thousand members; at a distance of two miles are founded two new communities. Till a general table shall be instituted, according to the fundamental constitution of the society, the members are placed in four boarding-houses, where they must live very frugally. Several of the most turbulent, with an Irishman who wore a long beard, at their head, wished to leave the society immediately to go to Mexico, there to settle themselves, but where their subsistence will be procured with as much difficulty.

In the evening Mr. Owen conducted me to a concert in the non-descript building. Most of the members of the society were present. The orchestra was not numerous, it consisted at first only of one violin, one violoncello, one clarionet and two flutes. Nevertheless the concert was surprisingly good, especially as the musicians have not been together a year. The clarionet player performed particularly well, and afterwards let us hear him on the bugle. Several good male and female vocalists then took a part, they sang among other things a trio accompanied by the clarionet only. Declamation was interspersed among the musical performances, Lord Byron's stanzas to his wife after their separation were extremely well recited. Between the two parts of the concert the music played a march, each gentleman gave a lady his arm, and a promenade took place, resembling a Polonaise with pretty figures, sometimes in two couples, sometimes in four; two ladies

*By late newspapers it appears that the society actually dissolved itself, in the beginning of the year 1827.

in the middle, the gentlemen separated from the ladies, then again all together. The concert closed with a lively cotillion. I was, on the whole, much amused; and Mr. Huygens took an active share in the dancing. This general evening amusement takes place often in the week; besides, on Tuesday, there is a general ball. There is a particular costume adopted for the society. That for the men consists of wide pantaloons buttoned over a boy's jacket, made of light material, without a collar; that of the women of a coat reaching to the knee and pantaloons, such as little girls wear among us. These dresses are not universally adopted, but they have a good appearance. An elderly French lady, who presides over the department of young mothers, and the nursing of all the very small children, stuck by my side during a large portion of the evening, and tormented me with her philosophical views. All the men did not take a share in the dance, i. e. the lower class, but read newspapers, which were scattered over the side-tables.

The public house in which we lived was conducted on account of the society. General Evans was looked for, who was to keep the house; in the mean time it was directed by the physician of the society, Dr. M'Namee, from Vincennes. Among the public buildings I remarked two of which the lower part was strongly built with rough stone, and provided with loop-holes. The larger of these was the granary, and it was reasonably thought that Rapp had this built as a defensive redoubt for his own people. At the first period of his establishment in this country he had not only had the Indians, but also the rude people known under the general title of backwoodsmen, who not only saw the establishment of such a society with jealous eyes, which they knew would be wealthy in a short time, but also entertained a grudge against Rapp's unnatural rules of chastity.

On the morning of the 14th of April, I strolled about the place to look round me. I visited Mr. Neef, but found his wife only at home, a native of Memmingen, in Swabia. Her husband was in the act of leading the boys out to labour. Military exercises form a part of the instruction of the children. I saw the boys divided into two ranks, and parted into detachments marching to labour, and on the way they performed various wheelings and evolutions. All the boys and girls have a very healthy look, are cheerful and lively, and by no means bashful. The boys labour in the field and garden, and were now occupied with new fencing. The girls learn female employments; they were as little oppressed as the boys with labour and teaching; these happy and interesting children were much more employed in making their youth pass as pleasantly as possible. Madam Neef showed the school-house, in which she dwelt, and in which the places for sleeping were arranged for the boys. Each boy slept on a cot frame, upon a straw bed.

We went next to Rapp's distillery: it will be removed altogether. Mr. Owen has forbidden distilling also, as well as the use of ardent spirits. Nothwithstanding this, the Irishmen here find opportunities of getting whiskey and fuddling themselves from the flat boats that stop here, &c. We saw also a dye-house and a mill set in motion by a steam-engine of ten horse-power. The engine was old and not in good order, Mr. Owen said however, he hoped to introduce steam-mills here in time from England. From the mills we went to the vineyard, which was enclosed and kept in very good order. I spoke to an old French vine-dresser here. He assured me that Rapp's people had not understood the art of making wine; that he would in time make more and much better wine, than had been done heretofore. The wine stocks are imported from the Cape of Good Hope, and the wine has an entirely and singular and strange taste, which reminds one of the common Spanish wines.

We went again to the quondam church, or workshop for the boys, who are intended for joiners and shoemakers. These boys sleep upon the floor above the church in cribs, three in a row, and thus have their sleeping place and place of instruction close together. We also saw the shops of the shoemakers, tailors and saddlers, also the smiths, of which six were under one roof, and the pottery, in which were two rather large furnaces. A porcelain earth has been discovered on the banks of the Mississippi, in the state of Illinois, not far from St. Louis. Two experienced members of the society, went in that direction, to bring some of the earth to try experiments with, in burning. The greater part of the young girls, whom we chanced to meet at home, we found employed in plaiting straw hats. I became acquainted with a Madam F—, a native of St. Petersburg. She married an American merchant, settled there, and had the misfortune to lose her husband three days after marriage. She then joined her husband's family at Philadelphia, and as she was somewhat eccentric and sentimental, quickly became enthusiastically attached to Mr. Owen's system. She told, me however, in German, that she found herself egregiously deceived; that the highly vaunted equality was not altogether to her taste; that some of the society were too low, and the table was below all criticism. The good lady appeared to be about to run from one extreme to the other for she added, that in the summer, she would enter a Shaker establishment near Vincennes.*

I renewed acquaintance here with Mr. Say, a distinguished naturalist from Philadelphia, whom I had been introduced to, at the Wistar Party there; unfortunately he had found himself embarrassed in his fortune, and was obliged to come here as a friend of Mr. M'Clure. This gentleman appeared quite comical in the costume of the society, before described, with his hands full of hard lumps and blisters, occasioned by the unusual labour he was obliged to undertake in the garden.

In the evening I went to walk in the streets, and met with several of the ladies of the society, who rested from the labours of the day. Madam F— was among them, whose complaints of disappointed expectations I had listened to. I feared still more from all that I saw and heard, that the society would have but a brief existence. I accompanied the ladies to a dancing assembly, which was held in the kitchen of one of the boarding-houses. I observed that this was only an hour of instruction to the unpractised in dancing, and that there was some restraint on account of my presence, from politeness I went away, and remained at home the remainder of the evening. About ten o'clock, an alarm of fire was suddenly raised. An old log building used as a washhouse was in flames, immediately the fire-engine kept in a distinct house, was brought and served by persons appointed to that duty. They threw the stream of water through the many apertures of the log-house, and quickly put a stop to the fire. In a quarter of an hour, all was over. Since the houses in the place all stand separately, there is nothing to fear from the extension of fire, unless in a strong wind. The houses, however, are all covered with shingles.

On the 15th of April, I went into the garden back of Rapp's house to see a plate or block of stone, which is remarkable as it bears the impression of two human feet. This piece of stone was hewed out of a rock near St. Louis, and sold to Mr. Rapp. Schoolcraft speaks of it in his travels, and I insert his remarks, as I have found them correct. "The impressions are to all appearance

*[According to the report of some females, who were induced to visit New Harmony, and remained there for some time, any situation much above abject wretchedness, was preferable to this vaunted terrestrial paradise.]—TRANS.

those of a man standing upright, the left foot a little forwards, the heels turned inwards. The distance between the heels by an exact measurement was six and a quarter inches, and thirteen and a half between the extremities of the great toes. By an accurate examination, it will however be ascertained, that they are not the impression of feet, accustomed to the use of European shoes, for the toes are pressed out, and the foot is flat, as is observed in persons who walk barefoot. The probability that they were caused by the pressure of an individual, that belonged to an unknown race of men, ignorant of the art of tanning hides, and that this took place in a much earlier age than the traditions of the present Indians extend to, this probability I say, is strengthened by the extraordinary size of the feet here given. In another respect, the impressions are strikingly natural, since the muscles of the feet are represented with the greatest exactness and truth. This circumstance weakens very much the hypothesis, that they are possibly evidences of the ancient sculpture of a race of men living in the remote ages of this continent. Neither history nor tradition, gives us the slightest information of such a people. For it must be kept in mind, that we have no proof that the people who erected our surprising western tumuli, ever had a knowledge of masonry, even much less of sculpture, or that they had invented the chisel, the knife, or the axe, those excepted made from porphyry, hornstone or obsidian. The medium length of the human male foot can be taken at ten inches. The length of the foot stamp here described, amounts to ten and a quarter inches, the breadth measured over the toes, in a right angle with the first line is four inches, but the greatest spread of the toes is four and a half inches, which breadth diminished at the heels to two and a half inches. Directly before these impressions is a well inserted and deep mark, similar to a scroll of which the greatest length is two feet seven inches, and the greatest breadth twelve and a half inches. The rock which contains these interesting traces, is a compact limestone of a bluish-gray colour."

This rock with the unknown impressions are remembered as long as the country about St. Louis has been known, this table is hewn out of a rock, and indeed out of a perpendicular wall of rock.

The garden of Rapp's house was the usual flower-garden of a rich German farmer. In it was a green-house, in which several large fig trees, an orange, and lemon tree stood in the earth. Mr. Owen took me into one of the newly-built houses, in which the married members of the society are to dwell. It consisted of two stories, in each two chambers and two alcoves, with the requisite ventilators. The cellar of the house is to contain a heating apparatus, to heat the whole with warm air. When all shall be thoroughly organized, the members will alternately have the charge of heating the apparatus. Each family will have a chamber and an alcove, which will be sufficient, as the little children will be in the nursery, and the larger at school. They will not require kitchens, as all are to eat in common. The unmarried women will live together, as will also the unmarried men, in the manner of the Moravian brethern.

I had an ample conversation with Mr. Owen, relating to his system, and his expectations. He looks forward to nothing less than to remodel the world entirely; to root out all crime; to abolish all punishments; to create similar views and similar wants, and in this manner to avoid all dissension and warfare. When his system of education shall be brought into connection with the great progress made by mechanics, and which is daily increasing every man can then, as he thought, provide his smaller necessaries for himself, and trade would cease entirely! I expressed a doubt of the practicability of his system in Europe, and even in the United States. He was too unalterably convinced of the results, to admit the slightest room for doubt. It grieved me to see that Mr. Owen should allow himself to be so infatuated by his passion for universal improvement, as to believe and to say that he is about to reform the whole world; and yet that almost every member of his society, with whom I have conversed apart, acknowledged that he was deceived in his expectations, and expressed their opinion that Mr. Owen had commenced on too grand a scale, and had admitted too many members, without the requisite selection! The territory of the society may contain twenty five thousand acres. The sum of one hundred and twenty thousand dollars was paid to Rapp for this purchase, and for that consideration he also left both his cattle, and a considerable flock of sheep behind.

I went with the elder Doctor M'Namee, to the two new established communities, one of which is called No. 2, or Macluria; the other lately founded, No. 3. No. 2, lies two miles distant from New Harmony, at the entrance of the forest, which will be cleared to make the land fit for cultivation, and consists of nine log houses, first tenanted about four weeks since, by about eighty persons. They are mostly backwoodsmen with their families, who have separated themselves from the community No. 1, in New Harmony, because *no religion* is acknowledged there, and these people wish to hold their prayer meetings undisturbed. The fields in the neighbourhood of this community were of course very new. The community No. 3, consisted of English country people, who formed a new association, as the mixture, or perhaps the cosmopolitism of New Harmony did not suit them; they left the colony planted by Mr. Birkbeck, at English Prairie, about twenty miles hence, on the right bank of the Wabash, after the unfortunate death of that gentleman,* and came here. This is a proof that there are two evils that strike at the root of the young societies; one is a sectarian or intolerant spirit; the other, national prejudice. No. 3, is to be built on a very pretty eminence, as yet there is only a frame building for three families begun.

After we had returned to New Harmony, I went to the orchard on the Mount Vernon road to walk, and beheld, to my great concern, what ravages the frost had committed on the fruit blossoms, the vines must have been completely killed. The orchards planted by Rapp and his society are large and very handsome, containing mostly apple and peach trees, also some pear and cherry trees. One of the gardens is exclusively devoted to flowers, where, in Rapp's time, a labyrinth was constructed of beech tree hedges and flowers, in the middle of which stood a pavilion, covered with the tops of trees.

I afterwards visited Mr. Neef, who is still full of the maxims and principles of the French revolution; captivated with the system of equality; talks of the emancipation of the negroes, and openly proclaims himself an ATHEIST. Such people stand by themselves, and fortunately are so very few in number, that they can do little or no injury.

In the evening there was a general meeting in the large hall, it opened with music. Then one of the members, an English architect of talent, who came to the United States, with Mr. Owen whose confidence he appeared to possess, and was here at the head of the arranging and architectural department, read some extracts from the newspapers, upon which Mr. Owen made a very good commentary; for example, upon the extension and improvement of steam-engines, upon their adaptation to navigation, and the advantages resulting therefrom. He lost himself, however, in his theories, when he expatiated on an article which related to

*He was drowned in the Wabash, which he attempted to swim over on horseback.

the experiments which had been made with Perkins's steam-gun. During these lectures, I made my observations on the much vaunted equality, as some tatterdemalions stretched themselves on the platform close by Mr. Owen. The better educated members kept themselves together, and took no notice of the others. I remarked also, that the members belonging to the higher class of society had put on the new costume, and made a party by themselves. After the lecture the band played a march, each gentleman took a lady, and marched with her round the room. Lastly, a cotillion was danced: the ladies were then escorted home, and each retired to his own quarters.

I went early on the following morning, (Sunday,) to the assembly room. The meeting was opened by music. After this Mr. Owen stated a proposition, in the discussion of which he spoke of the advance made by the society, and of the location of a new community at Valley Forge, in Pennsylvania, and another in the state of New York. A classification of the members was spoken of afterwards. They were separated into three classes, first, of such as undertook to be security for the sums due Mr. Owen and Mr. M'Clure, (that is, for the amount paid to Rapp, and so expended as a pledge to be redeemed by the society,) and who, if desirous to leave the society, must give six months previous notice; secondly, of such as after a notice of fourteen days can depart; and, lastly, of those who are received only on trial.

After this meeting, I paid Mr. M'Clure a visit, and received from him the French papers. Mr. M'Clure is old, childless, was never married, and intends, as is reported, to leave his property to the society. Afterwards I went with Mr. Owen, and some ladies of the society, to walk to the cut-off, as it is called, of the Wabash, where this river has formed a new channel, and an island, which contains more than a hundred acres of the best land; at present, however, inundated by water. There is here a substantial grist-mill, erected by Rapp, which was said to contain a very good set of machinery, but where we could not reach it on account of the water. We went some distance along the river, and then returned through the woods over the hills, which, as it was rather warm, and we could discover no pathway, was very laborious to the ladies, who were uncommonly alarmed at the different snakes we chanced to meet. Most of the serpent species here are harmless, and the children catch them for playthings. The poisonous snakes harbouring about here, are rattlesnakes and copperheads; these, however, diminish rapidly in numbers, for it is a common observation, that the poisonous serpents, like the Indians and bears, fly before civilization. The rattlesnakes have a powerful enemy in the numerous hogs, belonging to the settlers, running about the woods, which are very well skilled in catching them by the neck and devouring them.

In the evening I paid visits to some ladies, and witnessed philosophy and the love of equality put to the severest trial with one of them. She is named Virginia, from Philadelphia; is very young and pretty, was delicately brought up, and appears to have taken refuge here on account of an unhappy attachment. While she was singing and playing very well on the piano forte, she was told that the milking of the cows was her duty, and that they were waiting unmilked. Almost in tears, she betook herself to this servile employment, deprecating the new social system, and its so much prized equality.

After the cows were milked, in doing which the poor girl was trod on by one, and daubed by another, I joined an aquatic party with the young ladies and some young philosophers, in a very good boat upon the inundated meadows of the Wabash. The evening was beautiful moonlight, and the air very mild; the beautiful Miss Virginia forgot her *stable* sufferings, and regaled us with her sweet voice. Somewhat later we collected together in the house No. 2, appointed for a school-house, where all the young ladies and gentlemen of *quality* assembled. In spite of the equality so much recommended, this class of persons will not mix with the common sort, and I believe that all the well brought up members are disgusted, and will soon abandon the society. We amused ourselves exceedingly during the whole remainder of the evening, dancing cotillions, reels and waltzes, and with such animation as rendered it quite lively. New figures had been introduced among the cotillions, among which is one called the *new social system*. Several of the ladies made objections to dancing on Sunday; we thought however, that in this sanctuary of philosophy, such prejudices should be utterly discarded, and our arguments, as well as the inclination of the ladies, gained the victory.

On the 17th April, a violent storm arose, which collected such clouds of dust together that it was hardly possible to remain in the streets, and I remained at home almost all day. I received a visit from a Mr. Von Schott. This person, a Wurtemburger by birth, and brother of lady Von Mareuil, in Washington, has settled himself seven or eight miles from New Harmony, and lives a real hermit's life, without a servant or assistant of any kind. He was formerly an officer in the Wurtemberg cavalry, took his discharge, and went, from pure enthusiasm, and over-wrought fanaticism, to Greece, to defend their rights. As he there discovered himself to be deceived in his anticipations, he returned to his native country, and delivered himself up to religious superstition. To extricate himself, in his opinion, from this world plunged in wretchedness, he accompanied his sister to the United States, came to Indiana, bought a piece of land from Rapp, by whom he asserted he was imposed upon, and had difficulties to undergo, since he knew nothing of agriculture. He lived in this manner in the midst of the forest with a solitary horse. A cruel accident had befallen him the week before, his stable with his trusty horse was burnt. He appeared to be a well-informed man, and spoke well and rationally, only when he touched upon religious topics, his mind appeared to be somewhat deranged. He declared that he supported all possible privations with the greatest patience, only he felt the want of intercourse with a friend in his solitude.

To-day two companies of the New Harmony militia, paraded with drums beating, and exercised morning and afternoon. They were all in uniform, well armed, and presented an imposing front.

I was invited to dinner in the house, No. 4. Some gentlemen had been out hunting, and had brought home a wild turkey, which must be consumed. This turkey formed the whole dinner. Upon the whole I cannot complain either of an overloaded stomach or a head-ache from the wine affecting it, in any way. The living was frugal in the strictest sense, and in nowise pleased the elegant ladies with whom I dined. In the evening I visited Mr. M'Clure and Madam Fretageot, living in the same house. She is a Frenchwoman, who formerly kept a boarding-school in Philadelphia, and is called *mother* by all the young girls here. The handsomest and most polished of the female world here, Miss Lucia Saistare and Miss Virginia, were under her care. The cows were milked this evening when I came in, and therefore we could hear their performance on the piano forte, and their charming voices in peace and quiet. Later in the evening we went to the kitchen of No. 3, where there was a ball. The young ladies of the better class kept themselves in a corner under Madam Fretageot's protection, and formed a little aristocratical club. To prevent all possible partialities, the gentlemen as well as the ladies, drew numbers for the cotillion, and thus apportioned them equitably. Our young ladies turned up their noses apart at the democratic dancers, who often in this way fell to their lot. Although every one was pleased upon the whole, yet they separated at ten o'clock, as it is necessary to rise early here. I accompanied Madam Fretageot and her two pupils home, and passed some time in conversation with Mr. M'Clure on his travels in Europe, which were undertaken with mineralogical views. The architect, Mr. Whitwell, besides showed me to-day the plan of this establishment. I admired particularly the judicious and economical arrangements for warming and ventilating the buildings, as well as the kitchens and laundries. It would indeed be a desirable thing could a building on this plan once be completed, and Mr. Owen hopes that the whole of New Harmony will thus be arranged.

On the following day I received a visit from one of the German patriots who had entered the society, of the name of Schmidt, who wished to have been considered as first lieutenant in the Prussian artillery, at Erfurt. He appeared to have engaged in one of the political conspiracies there, and to have deserted. Mr. Owen brought him from England last autumn as a servant. He was now a member of the society, and had charge of the cattle. His fine visions of freedom seemed to be very much lowered, for he presented himself to me, and his father to Mr. Huygens, to be employed as servants.

Towards evening, an Englishman, a friend of Mr. Owen, Mr. Applegarth, arrived, who had presided over the school in New Lanark, and was to organize one here in all probability. After dinner I went to walk with him in the vineyard and woods. We conversed much concerning the new system, and the consequences which he had reason to expect would result, &c. and we discovered amongst other things, that Mr. Owen must have conceived the rough features of his general system from considering forced services or statutory labour; for the labour imposed upon persons for which they receive no compensation, would apply and operate much more upon them for their lodging, clothing, food, the education and care of their children, &c. so that they would consider their labour in the light of a corvèe. We observed several labourers employed in loading bricks upon a cart, and they performed this so tedious and disagreeable task, as a statutory labour imposed on them by circumstances, and his observation led us to the above reflection. I afterwards visited Mr. M'Clure, and entertained myself for an hour with the instructive conversation of this interesting old gentleman. Madam Fretageot, who appears to have considerable influence over Mr. M'Clure took an animated share in our discourse. In the evening there was a ball in the large assembly room, at which most of the members were present. It lasted only until ten o'clock, in dancing cotillions, and closed with a grand promenade, as before described. There was a particular place marked off by benches for the children to dance on, in the centre of the hall, where they could gambol about without running between the legs of the grown persons.

On the 19th of April, a steam-boat came down the Wabash, bound for Louisville on the Ohio. It stopt opposite Harmony, and sent a boat through the overflow of water to receive passengers. I was at first disposed to embrace the opportunity of leaving this place, but as I heard that the boat was none of the best, I determined rather to remain and go by land to Mount Vernon, to wait for a better steam-boat there. We took a walk to the community No. 3. The work on the house had made but little progress; we found but one workman there, and he was sleeping quite at his ease. This circumstance recalled the observation before mentioned, concerning gratis-labour, to my mind. We advanced beyond into the woods, commencing behind No. 3: there was still little verdure to be seen.

On the succeeding day, I intended to leave New Harmony early; but as it was impossible to procure a carriage, I was obliged to content myself. I walked to the community No. 2, or Macluria, and farther into the woods. They were employed in hewing down trees to build log houses. The wood used in the brick and frame houses here is of the tulip tree, which is abundant, worked easily, and lasts long. After dinner I walked with Mr. Owen and Madam Fretageot, to community No. 3. There a new vegetable garden was opened; farther on they were employed in preparing a field in which Indian corn was to be sown. This answers the best purpose here, as the soil is too rich for wheat; the stalks grow too long, the heads contain too few grains, and the stalks on account of their length soon break down, so that the crop is not very productive. The chief complaint here is on account of the too great luxuriancy of the soil. The trees are all very large, shoot up quickly to a great height, but have so few, and such weak roots, that they are easily prostrated by a violent storm; they also rot very easily, and I met with a great number of hollow trees, in proportion. I saw them sow maize or Indian corn, for the first time. There were furrows drawn diagonally across the field with the plough, each at a distance of two feet from the other;

then other furrows at the same distance apart, at right angles with the first. A person goes behind the plough with a bag of corn, and in each crossing of the furrows he drops six grains. Another person with a shovel follows, and covers these grains with earth. When the young plants are half a foot high, they are ploughed between and the earth thrown up on both sides of the plants; and when they are two feet high this operation is repeated, to give them more firmness and to destroy the weeds. There is a want of experienced farmers here; the furrows were badly made, and the whole was attended to rather too much *en amateur*.

After we returned to Madam Fretageot's, Mr. Owen showed me two interesting objects of his invention; one of them consisted of cubes of different sizes, representing the different classes of the British population in the year 1811, and showed what a powerful burden rested on the labouring class, and how desirable an equal division of property would be in that kingdom. The other was a plate, according to which, as Mr. Owen asserted, each child could be shown his capabilities, and upon which, after a mature self-examination, he can himself discover what progress he has made. The plate has this superscription: scale of human faculties and qualities at birth. It has ten scales with the following titles: from the left to the right, self-attachment; affections; judgment; imagination; memory; reflection; perception; excitability; courage; strength. Each scale is divided into one hundred parts, which are marked from five to five. A slide that can be moved up or down, shows the measure of the qualities therein specified each one possesses, or believes himself to possess.

I add but a few remarks more. Mr. Owen considers it as an absurdity to promise never-ending love on marriage. For this reason he has introduced the civil contract of marriage, after the manner of the Quakers, and the French laws into his community, and declares that the bond of matrimony is in no way indissoluble. The children indeed, cause no impediment in case of a separation, for they belong to the community from their second year, and are all brought up together.

Mr. M'Clure has shown himself a great adherent of the Pestalozzian system of education. He had cultivated Pestalozzi's acquaintance when upon his travels, and upon this recommendation brought Mr. Neef with him to Philadelphia, to carry this system into operation. At first it appeared to succeed perfectly, soon however, Mr. Neef found so many opposers, apparently on account of his anti-religious principles, that he gave up the business, and settled himself on a farm in the woods of Kentucky. He had just abandoned the farm to take the head of a boarding-school, which Mr. M'Clure intended to establish in New Harmony. Mr. Jennings, formerly mentioned, was likewise to co-operate in this school; his reserved and haughty character was ill suited for such a situation, and Messrs. Owen and M'Clure willingly consented to his withdrawing, as he would have done the boarding-school more injury, from the bad reputation in which he stood, than he could have assisted it by his acquirements. An Englishman by birth, he was brought up for a military life; this he had forsaken to devote himself to clerical pursuits, had arrived in the United States as a Universalist preacher, and had been received with much attention in that capacity in Cincinnati, till he abandoned himself with enthusiasm to the *new social system*, and made himself openly and publicly known as an ATHEIST.*

I passed the evening with the amiable Mr. M'Clure and Madam Fretageot, and became acquainted through them, with a French artist, Mons. Lesueur, calling himself uncle of Miss Virginia, as also a Dutch physician from Herzogenbusch, Dr. Troost, an eminent naturalist. Both are members of the community, and have just arrived from a scientific pedestrian tour to Illinois and the southern part of Missouri, where they have examined the iron, and particularly the lead-mine works, as well as the peculiarities of the different mountains. Mr. Lesueur has besides discovered several species of fish, as yet undescribed. He was there too early in the season to catch many snakes. Both gentlemen had together collected thirteen chests of natural curiosities, which are expected here immediately. Mr. Lesueur accompanied the naturalist Perron, as draftsman in his tour to New South Wales, under Captain Baudin, and possessed all the illuminated designs of the animals which were discovered for the first time on this voyage, upon vellum. This collection is unique of its kind, either as regards the interest of the objects represented, or in respect to their execution; and I account myself fortunate to have seen them through Mr. Lesueur's politeness. He showed me also the sketches he made while on his last pedestrian tour, as well as those during the voyage of several members of the society to Mount Vernon, down the Ohio from Pittsburgh. On this voyage, the society had many difficulties to contend with, and

*[He is at this time advertising a boarding school in the western country, on his own account, which is to be under his immediate superintendence.]—TRANS.

were obliged often to cut a path for the boat through the ice. The sketches exhibit the originality of talent of the artist. He had come with Mr. M'Clure in 1815, from France to Philadelphia, where he devoted himself to the arts and sciences. Whether he will remain long in this society or not, I cannot venture to decide.*

* * * From the want of a church in Mount Vernon, the meeting was held in the court-house. It was a temporary log-house, which formed but one room. The chimney fire, and two tallow candles formed the whole illumination of it, and the seats were constructed of some blocks and boards, upon which upwards of twenty people sat. The singing was conducted by a couple of old folks, with rather discordant voices. The preacher then rose, and delivered us a sermon. I could not follow his discourse well, and was very much fatigued by my day's walk. In his prayer, however, the minister alluded to those who despise the word of the Lord, and prayed for their conviction and conversion. This hint was evidently aimed at the community in New Harmony and the new social system. In the sermon there was no such allusion. Probably the discourse was one of those, which he knew by heart; which he delivered in various places, and admitted of no interpolations. The service lasted till ten o'clock at night.

* * * Eleven miles and a half higher, we saw Evansville upon an eminence upon the right shore, still an inconsiderable place, but busy; it being the principal place in the county of Vandeburg, in the state of Indiana, lying in the neighbourhood of a body of fertile land, and is a convenient landing place for emigrants, who go to the Wabash country. Upon the same shore are seen several dwellings upon the fresh turf, shaded by high green trees. Close below Evansville, a small river called Big Pigeon creek falls into the Ohio. In its mouth we saw several flat boats, with apparatus similar to pile-driving machines. These vessels belong to a contractor, who has entered into an engagement with the government, to make the Ohio free and clear of the snags and sawyers lying in its current. This work was discharged in a negligent manner, and the officer to whom the superintendence was committed, is censured for having suffered himself to be imposed upon.

*[He has left it some time since, as well as Dr. Troost.]—TRANS.

PART THREE

From *Diary and Recollections of Victor Colin Duclos.* Copied from the original manuscript by Mrs. Nora C. Fretageot, New Harmony, Ind.

DUCLOS, VICTOR COLIN.

Mr. Duclos came from France in 1823 at the age of five. In his recollections he describes his attendance at William Maclure's school in Philadelphia, the visit of Lafayette, and his departure for New Harmony to join the Owen colony in 1825. From Pittsburgh to Mt. Vernon, Ind., the trip was made by the Ohio River and the company is known as the "Boat load of knowledge." The passenger list included the names of Thomas Say, Charles A. Lesueur, Robert Dale Owen, Gerald Troost, Joseph Neff and Madame Fretageot. The account of New Harmony life is brought down to the year 1834.

I am a native of France and was born in Paris, May 22, 1818. I left there in the early part of the year 1823 with my aunt, Madam Marie D. Fretageot, to attend a School of Industry established by Mr. William Maclure in Philadelphia, Pa. We started from Havre in a sailing vessel in March, 1823, and were six weeks on the voyage. On board this vessel, who intended to make this school their home, were Madam Fretageot, her son Achilles E. Fretageot, a Swiss named Balthazar, Charles A. Lesueur, two French students, my brother, Peter L. Duclos, myself and several others. We arrived in New York in May, and went to Philadelphia in June. The school house was situated on the Schuylkill road about one mile from the city. It was a large fine brick building with a very large arched door in the centre. Surrounding the school building, were the most beautiful pleasure ground immaginable. This was William Maclure's "School of Industry."

In the year 1824, while at this school in Philadelphia, General Lafayette made his last visit to the United States. He visited our school, and in his review, all of us marched in single file in front of him, and he gently laid his hand on our heads and told us to be good boys. General Lafayette was a man about 5 ft. 9 in. in highth and spare built. His hair was long and very gray. He wore a black broadcloth frock coat. If the Almighty God should have dropped into the city at that time he could not have been more highly worshipped than was General Lafayette. This was about 76 years ago, and I imagine that I can to this day feel the gentle tap on my head from that noble man.

In the year 1824, Mr. Robert Owen, a gentleman from Scotland, purchased all of the interests of the Rapp Society in Posey County, Indiana, including the town of Harmonie where he, in a short time, founded the noted Owen Community. Somewhat later than this, William Maclure bought an interest in the property and concluded to remove his School of Industry to New Harmony from Philadelphia. Therefore the early part of the year 1825 was occupied in building a large keel boat at Pittsburgh, Pa. This boat being well fitted with rooms and otherwise properly arranged for the comfort of the passengers and crew, we moved to Pittsburgh by means of wagons and carriages. The boat contained the leading members of talent of the school, and was therefore styled the Boat load of knowledge, and named the Philanthropist.

In the fall of the year 1825 we started from Pittsburgh down the Ohio River to Mt Vernon, Ind. from thence to New Harmony. As well as I can remember the names of those on the boat, with incidental remarks concerning them, are about as follows:—

Madam Fretageot and son, A. E. Fretageot, Allan Ward, Mark Penrose, Phiquepal d' Arusmont—who afterwards married Francer Wright—Charles A. Lesueur, artist and naturalist, Thomas Say, naturalist, M. Chase, chemist, Mrs Chase, artist and musician, Cornelius Tiebout, artist and engraver, Miss Lucy Sistaire, and two sisters—Miss Lucy afterwards married Thomas Say—Virginia Dupalais and her brother, John Beal, wife and daughter Caroline—baby—William Maclure, Captain McDonald of the Isles, Balthazar, a Swiss, Charles Falque, Amedie Dufour, Peter L. Duclos, Victor C. Duclos, Miss Tiebout, age 10,—last five pupils of Phiquepal—Mr. Speakman and family, Robert Dale Owen, Gerard Troost, chemist and geologist, Robert Owen came part way with them. Mme. Fretageot was employed by Mr. Maclure to superintend the school, while the scientific gentlemen and some of the others were professors in the new School of Industry he was to establish at New Harmony

Cincinnati was the first place of importance at which we landed. There was at that time very few buildings between 3d street and the river. We traveled very slowly for the reason that we did not run the boat nights, and many delays were occasioned by the wind being too high for our boat to be handled.

During the trip while the boat was thus delayed, many of the party would spend their time in hunting, fishing and in scientific investigations. Fish and game abounded, so that a large portion of our subsistance was derived from these sources.

On reaching Louisville the weather was very windy and cold. Here we stopped for some time in order to find a "Falls pilot", to buy provisions, etc. In passing over the Falls we had a narrow escape from wrecking the boat. Soon after leaving Louisville, the ice came rushing down the river and pushed the boat out into the woods. Here we were compelled to stay three or four weeks. One of our party while out hunting broke his leg by falling off a rail fence, and two of the French students broke through the ice while skating and came near drowning. As soon as possible after the ice broke up, we launched our boat and continued our journey.

About the middle of January, 1826, we arrived at Evansville. At that time it was but little more than a flat-boat landing, the settlement consisting of a few small log cabins. On our arrival at Mt Vernon about the last week in January, 1826, we were transferred by wagons. Thus we finally reached our destination on the scene of the former home of the Rapp Society, the home of the new Owen Community, and the location of our new School of Industry.

To give some idea of the value and importance of the property belonging to the Rapp Society previous to the sale of Mr. Robert Owen, it is necessary to describe in detail the territory and the great amount of improvements, in building and in the productive and manufacturing interests of the society in the town and vacinity. During their occupancy, considering the short time in which this vast amount of work was performed the results were remarkable. Coming in 1814 and removing in 1824-5, beginning in the unbroken forest, in the short space of ten years they cleared about 4000 acres of land, built the town, containing comfortable homes of brick and frame, large granaries of wood and stone, oil mills, grist mills, sawmills, distilleries, and factories for the various branches of manufactures they engaged in.

The property consisted of about 3,000 acres of land surrounding and including the town site. This being on what is called the second bottom, a narrow strip of lower land between it and the river and stretching out into a wide low valley to the north, a range of hills on the south and east, and the low land of the Cut-off River to the west. Judging from the location of the principal buildings, the town was laid off in the form of a square, bordered by North, South, East and West Streets. The Main Street extended from the entrance of the Mt. Vernon wagon road to the foot of the hills north to North Street, with a wagon road from thence to the ferry landing on the Wabash River. One square west of Main Street was west Street, and to the east were Brewery and East Streets. The principal street leading east and west was Church Street, connecting on the east with the wagon road leading to Princeton and Evansville. North of Church were Granary and North Streets, to the south, Tavern, Steam Mill, and South Streets. The streets were named from the locations and after the buildings situated thereon. Thus Church St. from the old German Church, the old Fort or granary gave its name to Granary St. Brewery St. from the brewery, and so on.

In the town and surrounding suburbs there were a great many rudely constructed log cabins which were the homes of these industrious people in the first years of the settlement, many without floors and undoubtedly built for temporary use while the more substantial buildings were being erected. In the town limits were constructed about twenty substantial two story brick buildings, which with a few exceptions were built east and west on the corners of the blocks. There were about the same number of frame buildings two stories in heighth. The dwelling houses both frame and brick were built after the same design with the door opening into the yard, the houses being on the line of the streets, making the corners of the blocks. Most of the houses are still in use though the majority have been remodeled.

On the west of Brewery, between Church and Granary Sts. was a one story frame building about 30 x 60 ft. which was used as a hospital, now in use as a warehouse. On the north west corner of Main and Tavern streets was the Rapp Tavern, a two story frame about 30 x 60 ft fronting on Main Street. In the rear of this on Tavern Street was a two story brick of about the same dimensions. On the north of the brick was a large double porch in which was located the stairway for both buildings. In after years this property was used for many purposes and was known as the "White House," the upper and rear parts being used as a tenement house, now known as the Monitor Saloon, but in the early history of the town it was called the "Yellow Tavern". (Burned Aug. 1908)

Within the block east of Main and between Tavern and Church Sts. was a two story brick about 40 x 60 ft. built east and west, and within the block south of this was a building about 30 x 40 (still in use. 1902), the first story of stone, the second of brick. On the corner of Church and Brewery Sts. was a large frame livery stable. On the south east corner of Main and Church Sts. was a pit for whip-sawing the lumber first used in the construction of the buildings. These buildings were mostly used as dwellings for single families.

For school buildings the larger buildings were used. In reference to a class of buildings of special note that were numbered from 1 to 5, it is not definitely known what purpose they were constructed for. A study of position and internal arrangement, surroundings, etc. will offer some suggestions as to their use.

No. 1 stood east of West Street on the corner of West and Steam Mill Streets (N.E.) was a two story brick about 40 x 70 ft. with a hallway on both floors, the whole length of the building. Contained sixteen large rooms.

No. 2, on the east side of Main between Church and Granary Str. was a three story brick 40 x 70 ft. with a kind of mansard roof, two stories of brick and the third formed by the mansard roof. The entrance was on an alley opening into a hall extending from end to end, with rooms on both sides in each story opening into the hallways. East of this was a large building used for a kitchen.

No. 3 was situated about the center of the block on the south side of Church, between Main and Brewery Sts. similar in size and construction to No. 1. It is built off the line of the street about ten feet. Runs north and south, the entrance on Church Street.

No. 4, same as No. 1–3, on Church Street, North side between brewery and East Street.

No. 5 was the home of George Rapp, the founder of the society. It was located on the Northwest corner of Church and Main Streets, about 30 feet back from both streets. It was of brick, two stories in highth, with a one story ell on the west. The foundation was about four feet in highth, of dressed sandstone. A porch or verandah extended the whole length on the south and east sides, with large stone steps to each entrance. On each floor there were large halls leading east and west. This building was destroyed by fire about the year 1842, (1844), supposed to have been the work of an incendiary.

A few feet north of No. 5 was a large oak tree. Tradition tells us that this spot was the camping ground of those members of the society who were the first to spend the night in this locality, and ever after during their residence here, it was a favorite spot for the society band to meet and discourse sweet music.

The place of worship during the last few years of their residence here was a building constructed from plans of George Rapp and conceived by him in a dream. This was a two story brick building constructed in the year 1822, but the internal arrangement was never carried out. It stood on the northwest part of the block on Church Street between Main and West Streets. It was planned so that the interior at the pulpit represented a large cross. The dimensions of the centre square was about 40 feet, and each wing the same. (Mr. Dransfield has written in parenthesis "This is not exact as the wings were 50 feet in width, and the interior square was about 70 feet each way.") The centre roof was supported by four columns about eighteen inches in diameter and twenty-five feet in highth (really two feet in diameter), each turned by hand from one stick of timber, of cherry, poplar, or walnut. These columns stood on a large moulded base of the same wood, about forty feet in highth from the foundation. In the centre of the building was a large dome, encircling which was a balcony at times used as a band stand. The entrances to each wing were large stone foundations with the semi-circular stone steps. The second and third steps were moulded on the edge. The north door, which was the principal entrance, was of cherry. The doorway was of carved stone capped by a cornice terminating in a gable in the panel of which was carved a rose, gilded, with a reference to it taken from the Bible, carved in the stone. The other doorways were also of stone but more simply finished.

The old church built about 1815 stood east of this on the same lot and was a two story frame with six large arched windows on the sides, and two in the end, with round windows in the gables. A belfry 20 x 20 feet and 20 feet above the roof was built on the east end. This had large slatted windows in each side and contained one large and one small bell. A clock room, hexagonal in shape was built above the belfry. On the northeast of this was a clock face about eight feet in diameter, and a similar one on the southeast. Within this room was a clock gearing occupying a space of about six (ft?) square and the same in highth. This was arranged to strike the hours on the large bell and the small bell to note the quarter hours. These bells could be heard a distance of seven miles, and were the two finest ones in the state at that time. (went to Concinnati). The church steeple was built above the belfry.

As a protection against Indians and known as the Fort was a building 40 x 70 feet south of Granary between Main and West Streets. The first story was of rough stone, the walls about two feet in thickness with six port holes on either side and two on each end. The windows were barred with iron. The second and third stories were of brick. The two lower floors were laid with tile about nine inches square, probably with the object of preventing them being fired from the outside. The third story in the attic was floored with wood. The roof was what is known as a hipped roof and was very strongly built and covered with large tiles 7 x 12 inches, with hooks on the under side to lap over the lathing. There were three doorways, one on the north, south and east. The doors were very thick and strong and were securely fastened by enormous locks, and also barred as an additional security. At the south end of this was a kitchen with a subterranean passage way connecting the cellar with the interior of the Fort. But this has never been substantiated. (There was no cellar to this building, but when it was torn down to build the "new laboratory", a small arched chamber about six feet wide and eight feet long was found.)

On the same block, fronting on Church Street was a greenhouse about 20 x 40 feet, supported on rollers with lower foundation timbers twice the width of the house. On these were rails on which the grooved rollers travelled, allowing the building to be moved back and forth. In each side of the house was a liberal supply of glass windows, and the room was heated with the old style of tinplate stoves. Within this house were grown many kinds of tropical fruits, flowers, ferns, etc.

Within the same block and west of this was a press house, a one story frame about 30 x 36 feet. Here was located the cider and wine press, a large wooden screw with a large lever to operate it. The apples were reduced to pulp by a large circular stone pivoted in the centre. This stone was twelve inches in thickness and about six feet in diameter. It was revolved on a shaft and travelled in a circle probably twenty feet in diameter in a stone trough, in this the apples are shovelled and crushed by the revolving stone until in condition for the press.

The brickyard was at about the distance of two blocks south of South Street on the east side of the Mt. Vernon road near where Murphy Park is located.

West of this was the rope walk, west side of the road. This was not enclosed except to protect the machinery. Southwest of this and to the north of the road, leading to the Cutoff River was their Labyrinth. Within a circle of about 140 feet in diameter there were formed concentric circles with growth of hedge plants, presenting an intricate pathway leading to a small block house in the centre. The house was built of blocks of wood about twelve inches long pointed at one end. These were placed with the pointed ends outward to form a circular wall. The arrangement was such that it was almost impossible for anyone not accustomed to the construction to find their way to the building or to its interior.

At the northwest intersection of Brewery and North Streets was a frame building used for a brewery. In connection with this was a tread wheel built on a platform about twelve feet high. Within the wheel a dog or other small animal was used to furnish power to pump water.

On the south side of Steam Mill Street between Brewery and East Streets were two frame buildings about 40 x 45 feet, three stories high. The one to the west was used for a cotton mill, the other as a store house. The cotton mill was driven by steam power and contained a complete outfit of cotton manufacturing machinery. The mill was operated after the Germans left until destroyed by fire in 1826.

East of East Street between Tavern and Steam Mill Streets were two large three story frame hip-roofed granaries about 50 x 80 feet. In the attic of one of them was a large tread wheel about fourteen feet in diameter in which cattle or other heavy animals were used to create power for elevating grain.

Other buildings used for warehouses, etc. were located in different parts of the town. About forty acres of land west and south of the town were planted in orchards (nearer sixty) and vinyards. On the hills east of the Mt Vernon road was a large vinyard of about eighteen acres, and east of this large orchards. The sight of these orchards was enough to impress the mind of anyone of the ability and industry of this remarkable society.

South of the Labyrinth was a large locust grove. East of the Mt Vernon road were a number of log cabins. To the west of the road but on the hills were many black locust trees evidently set out to supply material for fence posts.

On my arrival here the only flouring mill in this locality was the one built by the Germans on the east bank and near the mouth of the Cut-off River about two miles southwest of town. The building was a three story frame. It was run by water power, containing four run of stones. About two miles southeast of town, located on Gresham Creek was an oil mill driven by water power. There was also a distillery on the same stream below and north of the Princeton road. Near this and east of the Creek were many log cabins. This was Community No. 2. No. 3 was west of the Creek at the foot of the hills.

When we arrived the scholars of the Maclore school went to the Neef boarding school in No. 2 until No. 5 was prepared for them. Then Madam Fretageot assumed controll as superintendent. In the No. 5 building painting, drawing, engraving and type-setting along with the common branches were taught. The painting and engraving department was in the assembly hall. In the old German frame church, with its belfry containing the town clock, shoe making was conducted on quite a large scale. In other buildings in the western and northern parts of the town, different branches of manufactures were conducted, so that the scholars could work at any trade they wished.

In No. 5 we would study from an early hour, frequently beginning at three A.M. until eight, and from one P.M. to three P.M. The remainder of the mornings and afternoons would be devoted to work at the various trades.

West of No. 5 was a building in which our meals were served. For breakfast we had an allowance of one and a half pints of milk, one large spoonful of molasses and as much corn meal mush as we wished. At noon we would have meat and vegetables, for supper we would return to mush and milk. At first we had coffee for breakfast but later Mme. Fretageot thought that was too extravagant, so henceforward we were only allowed coffee Sunday mornings. Two Mexican boys attended the school, who were sent from Mexico by William Maclure. James-Louis, aged 10, and Sevalla, 8. They could not speak English and when they wanted to know if the next day was Sunday they would say "Tomorrow coffee?" and if answered in the affirmative their joy would be unbounded. After the close of the school they were sent back to Mexico and a few years later Sevalla was killed by brigands while driving a stage coach near the City of Mexico. Louis was never heard from after his arrival in his native home.

The pupils would alternately assist in the kitchen, stirring the mush, preparing the vegetables, washing dishes, etc. also milk the cows and attend to the horses and other stock. An intermeddling Dutchman, named Kreutz, assisted in the care of the stock, whose overbearing ways made him very obnoxious to the boys who were daily brought in contact with him. One day I was out in the yard milking and was unfortunate enough to be kicked over by the cow who also as a parting act of good friendship, stepped on my foot which I resented by striking her three or four times with the milking stool. The Dutchman saw me tanning the cow and commenced abusing me. He also threatened to thrash me. I told him I would not milk another cow. He though I called him "A d—— old sow." He picked up a clapboard and started after me. I ran for the house yelling for help, as I reached the door the whole school was up greatly excited. They let me in and closed the door on my pursuer. The teacher wanted to know what it was all about. The Dutchman told her what he thought I had called him, but with a full explanation I came out all right.

A Swiss, named Baltazzar, a kind of an artist had a room in the south east corner of No. 2, and had made a large oil painting of the old Rapp church. It was hanging on the wall of his room and some of the boys decided that his lines were not perpendicular, so they drew on one side a number of men with poles against it to push it into position and a number on the opposite side pulling on ropes fastened to the eaves, pulling at it. When he saw what they had done he was so angry that he surely would have killed the guilty parties had he been able to find out who they were. Another trick played on Balthazzar (spelled several ways) was then he and Mike Craddock quarrelled. He sent Mike a challenge to fight a duel which was accepted and it was decided that pistols should be used, distance—five paces. Seconds were appointed who decided that blank cartridges should be used, and that Craddock should fall at the first fire. So early in the morning the parties repaired to a secluded spot in the old orchard and the men took their positions and glared at each other while the seconds carefully loaded the pistols. Tom Cox, one of the seconds, instructed the principals that the signal to fire should be the dropping of a handkerchief, and that the result of this fire should settle the matter. To this the principals agreed. Their weapons were handed them and the signal given. There was scarcely any difference in the reports of the two weapons. Balthazzar was apparently unhurt, but Craddock staggered, dropped his pistol, clapped his hand to his heart, and fell backward apparently dead. It was a most realistic performance. His seconds rushed up, opened his coat and pronounced him dead. Balthazzar was frightened almost to death. He cried "For God's sake, run for a doctor." At this Craddock burst out laughing. Balthazzar saw he was the victim of a practical joke, altho much chagrined, he was well satisfied as to the outcome. He was very sensitive over it when the subject was brought up and finally returned to Europe, and as he said "to the company of gentlemen."

One morning at the breakfast table we were all seated on a row of benches at either side of the table, and the mush placed near one of the rows so the scholars could help themselves. A young man, wishing more mush, lifted his foot over the seat and placed it down in the hot mush that happened to be directly behind him. He jumped about four feet high and yelled like a wild Indian, dancing over the floor he scattered the hot mush in every direction.

One of our teachers, Mr. Lesueur, was a fine artist. He taught drawing and painting, and did a great deal of artistic work outside of the school. He and Thomas Say spent most of their leisure in the woods or in the river searching for shells and catching fish which they painted and described. Mr. Lesueur also devoted some of his time to painting scenes for the Theatre. One notable scene on the south end of the old Hall was for the play of William Tell. It was still in good preservation when the building was torn down in 1874. It is related that one of his scenes represented a forest and the work was so artisticly executed that many of the audience thought they were real trees. The first piece put on the stage was The Maid and the Magpie. One scene represented a church with steeple and belfry. The maid arranged the table on the stage.

Mr. Lesueur constructed a magpie and operated it so that it flew down while the maid was absent and took a spoon from the table, up to its nest in the belfry, then returned and flew back with another spoon. The spoons were missed and the maid accused of the theft. After having been put on trial, she was condemned to death. The day of execution arrived. The executioner, supported by a double file of soldiers, marched in. The belfry man goes up in the belfry to toll the bell and finds the spoons in the magpie's nest. One of our teachers, Mrs Chase, took the part of the maid. About one year afterwards, Mr. Lesueur was called back to France by the French government and on his arrival there he was granted a large pension for valuable services rendered on various exploring expeditions.

One of our teachers was a copper plate engraver named Tiebout, who instructed the scholars in the art. Mrs Tiebout also taught in the schools. They had two children who were pupils, one, a daughter, about twelve years old who in later years married a man named Cologne, the other a son about nine. Mr. Tiebout died here and was buried in the Woods' graveyard.

Mr. Thomas Say was a fine gentleman and the scholars thought a great deal of him, in fact he was beloved by the whole community. I spent a part of almost every day at his home on the northwest corner of Granary and West Streets.

Our clothing was quite an item with us. The costume of the men and boys consisted of a jacket made quite large, pleated back and front with a band at the waist to which the pantaloons were buttoned. These were made to fit loosely and had no pockets. This formed our summer suit.

One summer, while in swimming, at the ford of Gresham Creek, where the old covered bridge spans the stream, with the other boys, I left my suit up on the bank and lingered in the water after the other boys had dressed and gone. When I came out I could not find my clothes. On looking around, a saw a cow about thirty yards off with something hanging from her mouth. I discovered it was a leg of my lost pants which she was trying to dispose of. So I put on my little jacket and chased her around the common until I managed to secure a hold on about six inches of the leg. I pulled them out but they were in a sad condition. I took them to the Creek and washed them out the best I could and put them on and went home. For a long time after that I went by the name of "chawed breeches."

About the year 1830, a young man named Oliver Evans came to town, and about a year later married Miss Louisa Neef, a daughter of one of our principal teachers. Mr Evans built a foundry north of North Street and east of Main. In connection with the foundry was a plow factory. Working on the building of the foundry, was a carpenter, named Chambers. He made a mortise on the wrong side of a stick of timber. He stood with his foot on the timber studying how to remedy the error, his elbow on his knee and his chin resting on his hand. A man coming up from the river noticed his preoccupied situation and asked him if he had the toothache, he said "yes", so the man said he would send Dr. Thompson down to pull it. The Doctor hastened down and found Chambers still resting as the man had found him. The Doctor asked him if he wanted it extracted he said "no" but he would like him to pull out this hole and put it on the other side of the timber. Dr. Thompson was very wrothy.

He said "yes, yes, Chalmers, I will make you pay for this", and sure enough, he did.

The Evans foundry made the first cast plows that were made in the state, but he found he could buy the castings in Pittsburgh for about what the pig iron would cost delivered in New Harmony.

The flouring mill at the Cutt-off was owned by Mr. Maclure and the miller was named Pennypacker. He was a man of great strength, and very proud of showing what he could do. One of his feats was to hang a 56 pound weight on his little finger and write his name with his arm extended full length. He would carry a barrel of flour under each arm. Mr. Pennypacker would come to the school to pay his rent. He frequently had to take two or three yoke of oxen and plow out the head of the Cut-off to get enough water to run the mill.

There was a fire engine left here by the Germans that was used for protection against fire. It was arranged to be worked by eighteen men and was supplied with water by buckets. It was made by Pat Lyon in Philadelphia about 1804 and is still in use by the town.

About 1834, a gentleman, Prince Maximillian, visited the town. He had with him three or four scientific men. He traveled under the name of Baron Brownsburg. While here he had a room in the northwest corner of No. 2, on the second floor. I was with him nearly every day and often accompanied him as a guide in his rambles over the country. Mr. B. asked me one day to get a skift and take him over on Fox Island. I did so, and fired his gun, frequently, but with poor success.

SKETCHES OF NEW HARMONY
BY
CHARLES ALEXANDRE LESUEUR

Reproduced by permission of the Museum d'Histoire Naturelle, Le Havre, which holds the original Lesueur sketches, and courtesy of the American Antiquarian Society who furnished copies of their photographs of Lesueur's American sketches. The sequence of presentation follows the enumeration and identification of R. W. G. Vail, "The American Sketchbooks of a French Naturalist," *American Antiquarian Society, Proceedings*, N.S., Vol. 48, Pt. 1 (Apr., 1938), pp. 49-155. The publishers note the uneven quality of the sketches which have been faithfully reproduced from available photographic copies.

SCENES IN AND AROUND NEW HARMONY, MAY, 1826.
Leland 131

222. [Unidentified and much blurred sketch of house]. May 17, 1826.
223. Harmony. [View from the Wabash, showing the town faintly outlined on the right bank]. May 17, 1826.
224. Wabash [near New Harmony]. May 17, 1826.
225. Bon Rèpos—dit Bon pos Creek sur le Wabash. [Two-story log house and outbuildings in clearing]. May 17, 1826.
226. From the piazza of M. [View down across a broad sweep of fields and woods, perhaps from the house of William Maclure at New Harmony]. 18 May 1826.
227. [Large two-story house with wide piazzas on both floors. Perhaps the house from which the preceding sketch was made]. 18 May 1826.
228. [Another view of the same house as 227]. 19 May 1826.
229. [Unidentified house within picket fence, with two story central part and one story wings on either side. Probably one of the original Rappist houses at New Harmony].
230. [Broad view of rolling fields and woodlands, similar to 226].
231. [Unidentified one-story house on hill among trees].
232. [Unidentified view from rustic porch of log house, looking down across rolling country to wooded river beyond. Dinner table with dishes on porch; seated woman with back to artist. Reproduced in *Dessins de Ch.–A. Lesueur, plate 48*, where it is incorrectly describe as the verandah of a house near New Orleans. It is more probably a view from a New Harmony home. Perhaps same as 864].
233. [Unidentified one-story log house with two wide porches with a dozen people on or near them. The house from which the preceding sketch was made]. 21 May.
234. [Unidentified sketch of four men and two horses working in a field, probably at New Harmony]. 22 May 1826.
235. [Unidentified sketch of open but flatter country from another porch].
236. [Unidentified one-story house with wide porch from which

the previous sketch was made]. 22 May.
237. [Unidentified square two-story house with wide porch and roof sloping to centre from all four sides; woman on knees planting flowers in foreground. Probably a Rappist house at New Harmony].
238. Depart de chez M. Polorne [?] [Six men and women about to set out on horseback].
239. [Three unidentified sketches, distant views of cleared land dotted with trees]. 25 May 1826.
240. [Unidentified picnic party of eight men and women seated under trees with four saddle horses at right and wagon with ox team at left]. 26 May au soir.
241. Vue de Harmony à notre arrivée sur le flat boat. [Two rough sketches of the town as seen from the Wabash River]. 27 May.
242. New Harmony. [Street scene with the old Rappist church and the Hall back of it. Reproduced in *Dessins de Ch.-A. Lesueur, plate 28* where it is dated May, 1826].

A NEW HARMONY BARBECUE IN 1832

The proper sequence of the following sketches is: 743, 744, 748, 745, 741, 742, 746.
741. Depart après le festin. [Departure after the feast. Two men shoving a boat into the Cut-off River, three-story mill on opposite bank of the stream. This barbecue was held by the people of New Harmony on Cut-off Island in the Wabash River opposite New Harmony at the mouth of the Cut-off River, about two miles from the town. On the Cut-off River near its mouth stands the old Rappist grist mill which appears in this picture]. *Leland 134.*
742. Depart & embarquement du vivre. [Departure and loading of the food. Three men loading two boats at the edge of the island at left, three others loading a small covered wagon at the right, in the background the remains of two large barbecue pits with frames of rails around them].

743. Arrivée & preparation du festin. [Men standing by a large tree from a limb of which hangs a hog with a pile of three or four large fish on the ground and with a pail of bottles in a hollow at the base of the tree.
744. Pecheurs. [Fishermen at the edge of the Cut-off River at the left of the old Rappist mill which stood on the east bank of the river near its mouth and two miles from New Harmony. This view from across the little river is beautifully drawn and is locally important since this was the mill which supplied the flour for New Harmony for many years. The scene is similar to No. 741 but better drawn].
745. Après le festin. [After the feast. View shows same hollow tree as in No. 743 with a dozen men sitting or standing about, one man and two jugs by the tree, a dozen more men visiting at right, one of them aiming a gun at a mark, three of the figures being drawn with sufficient care as to be recognizable].
746. Retour & entrée à N. H. [Procession led by man on horseback and consisting of two men with flag and gun, six men pulling the small covered wagon, eight men in single file, carrying fishpoles, the parade passing the old Rappist church with the Hall back of it].

Views of New Harmony

747. [Unidentified sketch of a cow grazing under a tree near an enclosure].
748. Barbaccue on Cut off I[s]land, N. H. 1832. [Four women working at a table under the trees with dogs and children about. This sketch belongs with the previous group]. *Leland 135.*
749. Hall & Lesueur house N. Hy. [Rear view of the Hall at left with Lesueur's house and garden at right]. *Hamy, p. 56*, redrawn by M. A. Noury, *Leland 131.*
750. [New Harmony, looking north on West Street with the Hall (old Rappist brick church) on right, small two-story house on left corner with large brick Rappist building back of it, facing the next street, and four or five other houses extending down West Street. Two

little girls are making mud pies in the middle of the street]. 15 Novembre à 4 heure 1831.
751. [View near New Harmony showing man sitting on log at top of high hill, looking off across the winding valley of the Wabash with New Harmony in the distance at the right of the river].
752. [Dooryard scene at New Harmony showing corner of large two-story house at left, with two people in the doorway, five women and a man seated below and a boy standing near, open woodland at right].
753. [Distant view of New Harmony seen through trees from the top of a hill, showing the Hall, the Rappist church and about 15 other buildings. View in the atlas of Maximilain's travels taken from the same point. Probably Lesueur and Bodmer, Maximilian's artist, climbed the hill and made their drawings together in 1833-4].
754. [Man driving span of oxen with large farm wagon with solid wooden wheels, sketched in front of tavern with sign hanging from pole at left, a two-story house and three smaller buildings across the street]. 1 Octobre 1826.

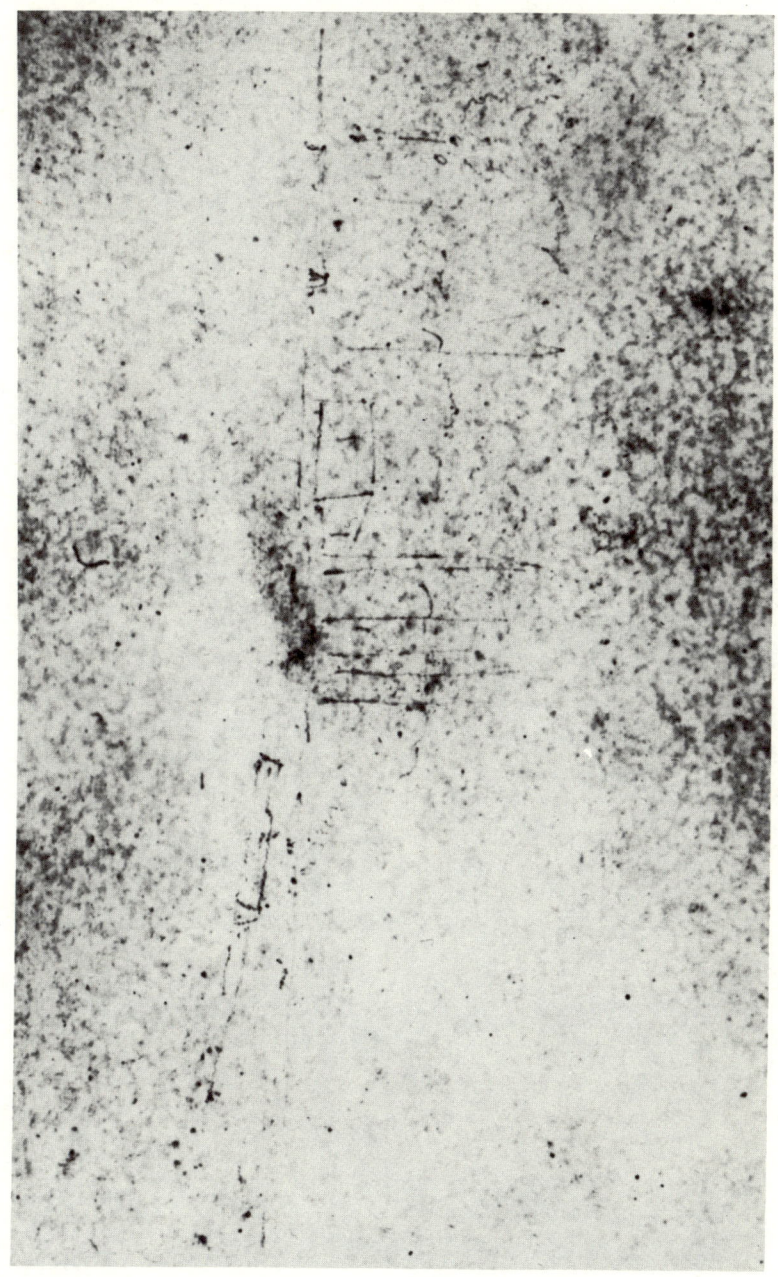

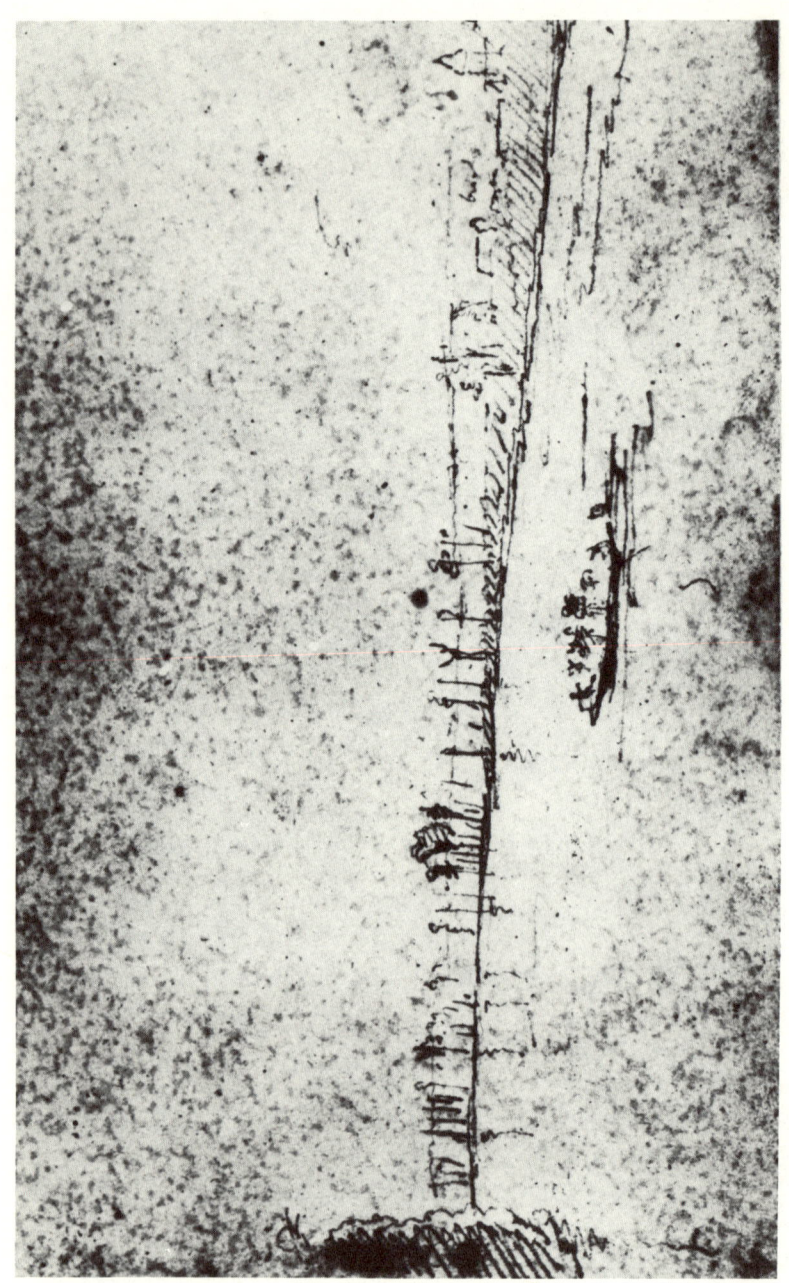

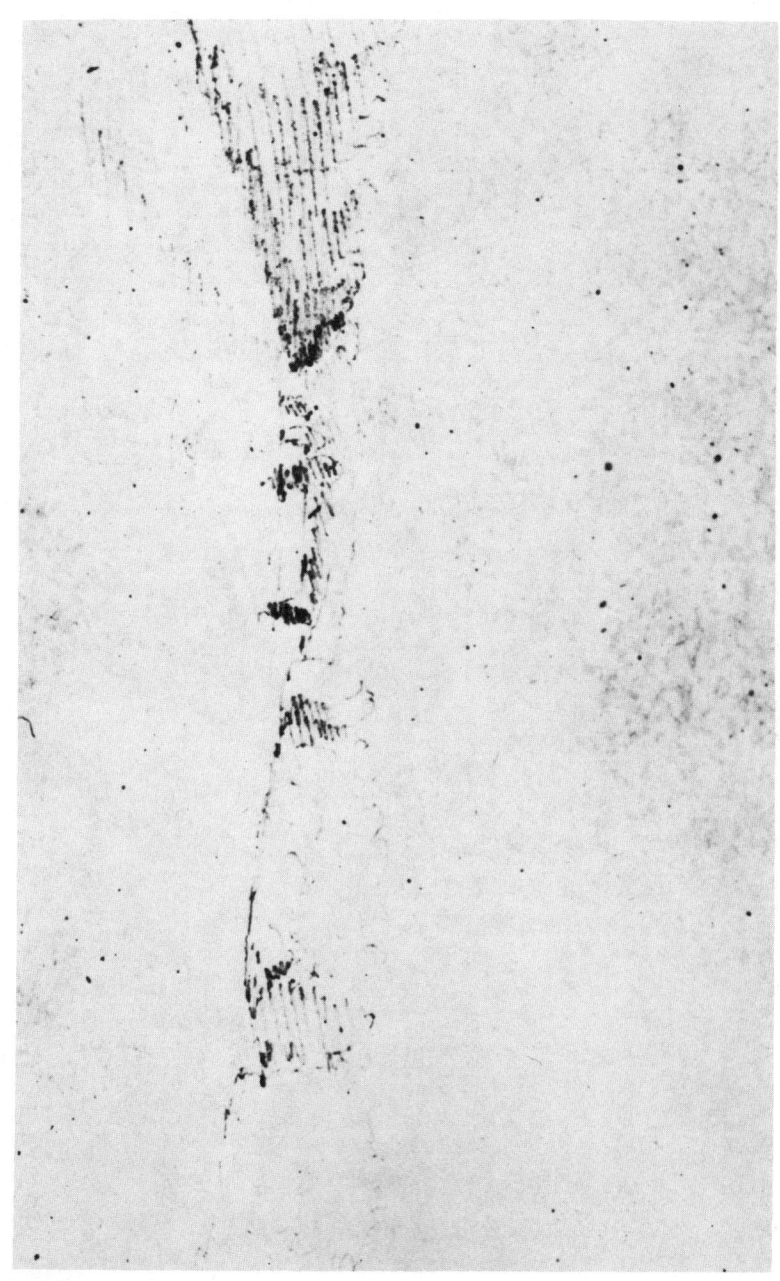

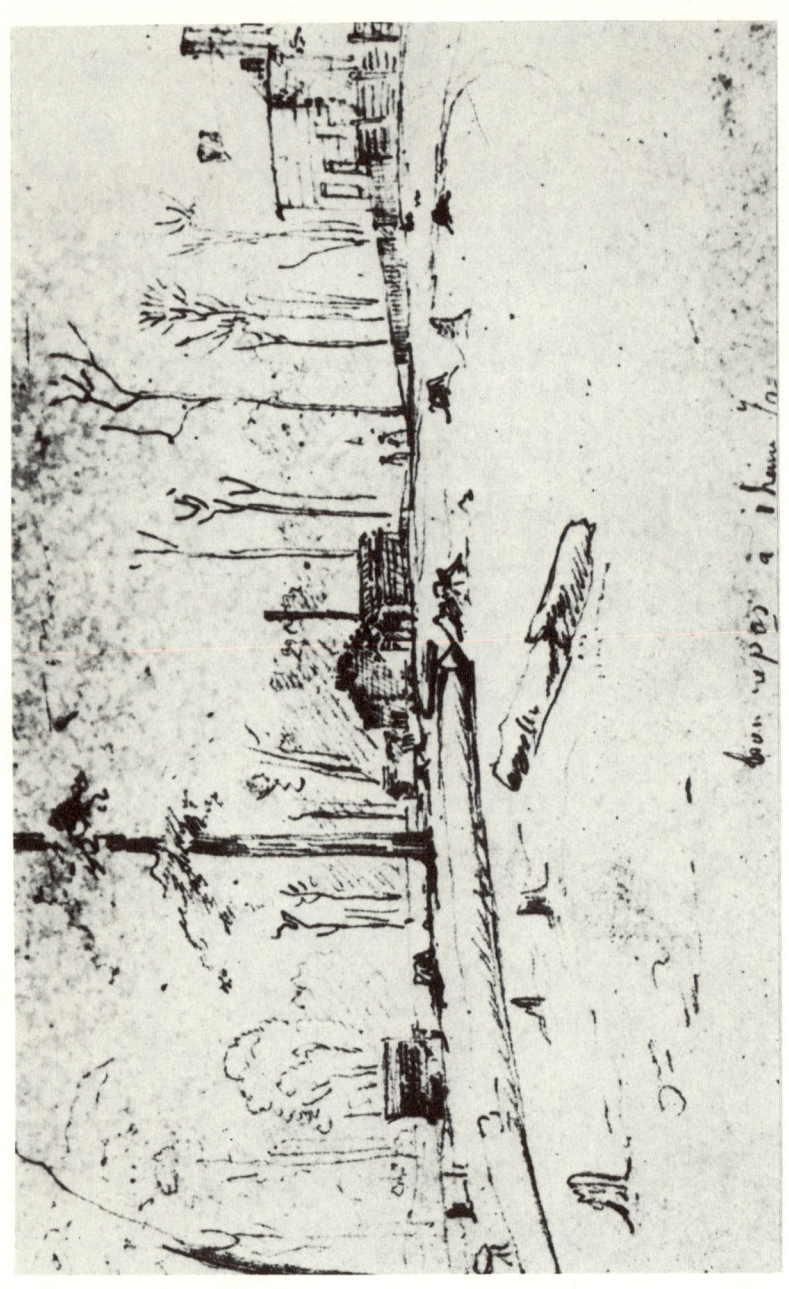

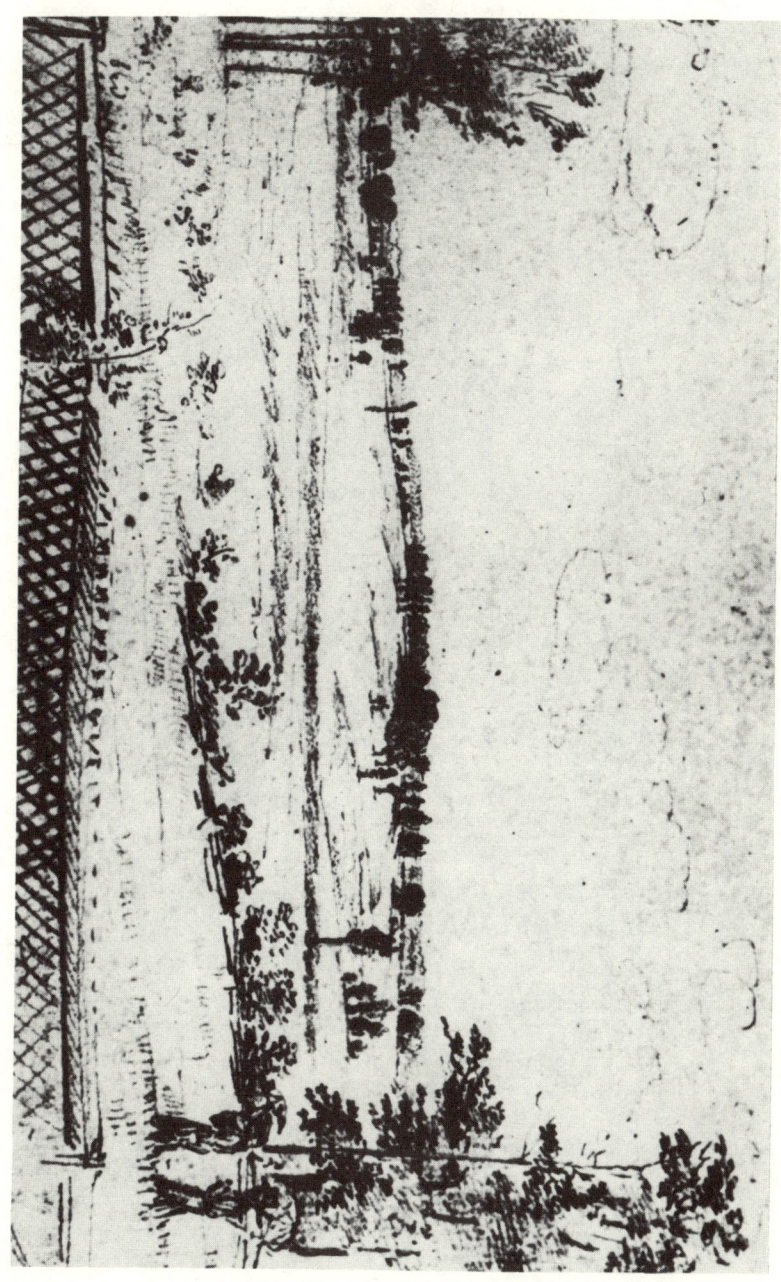

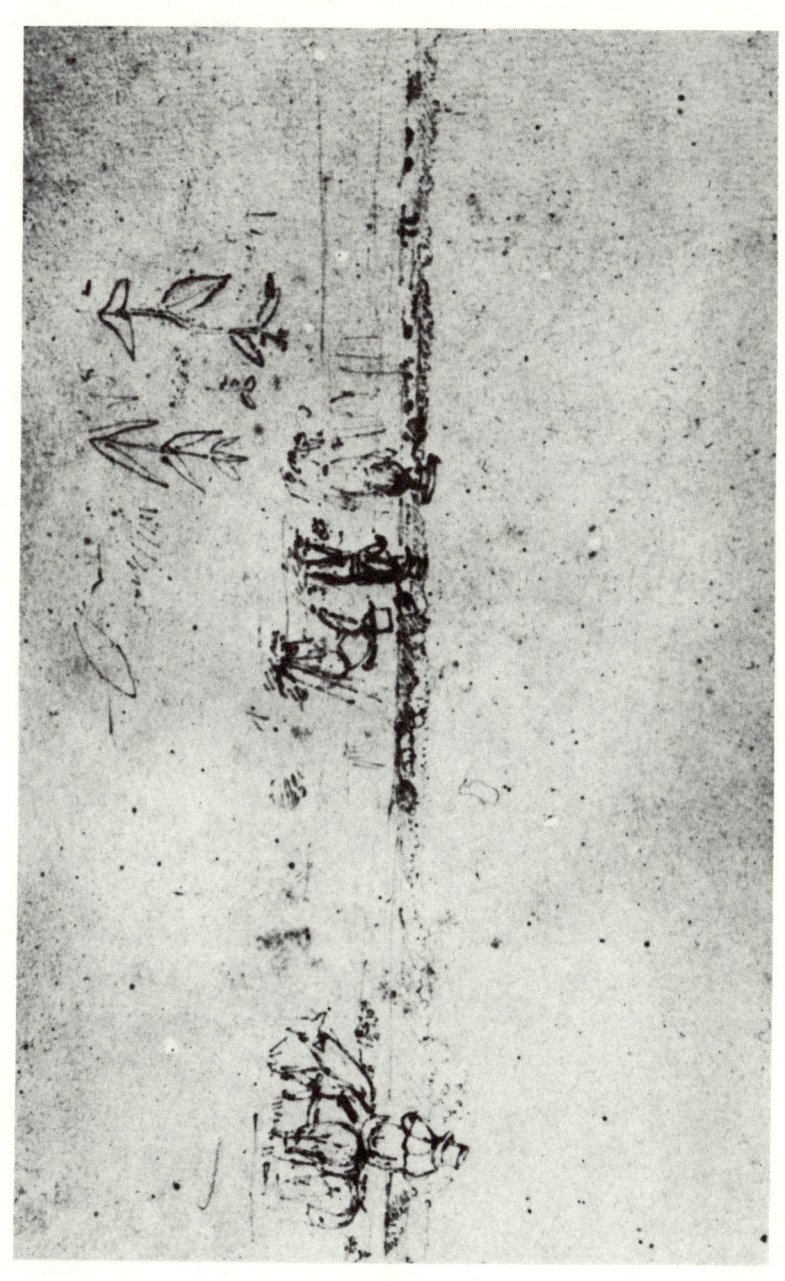

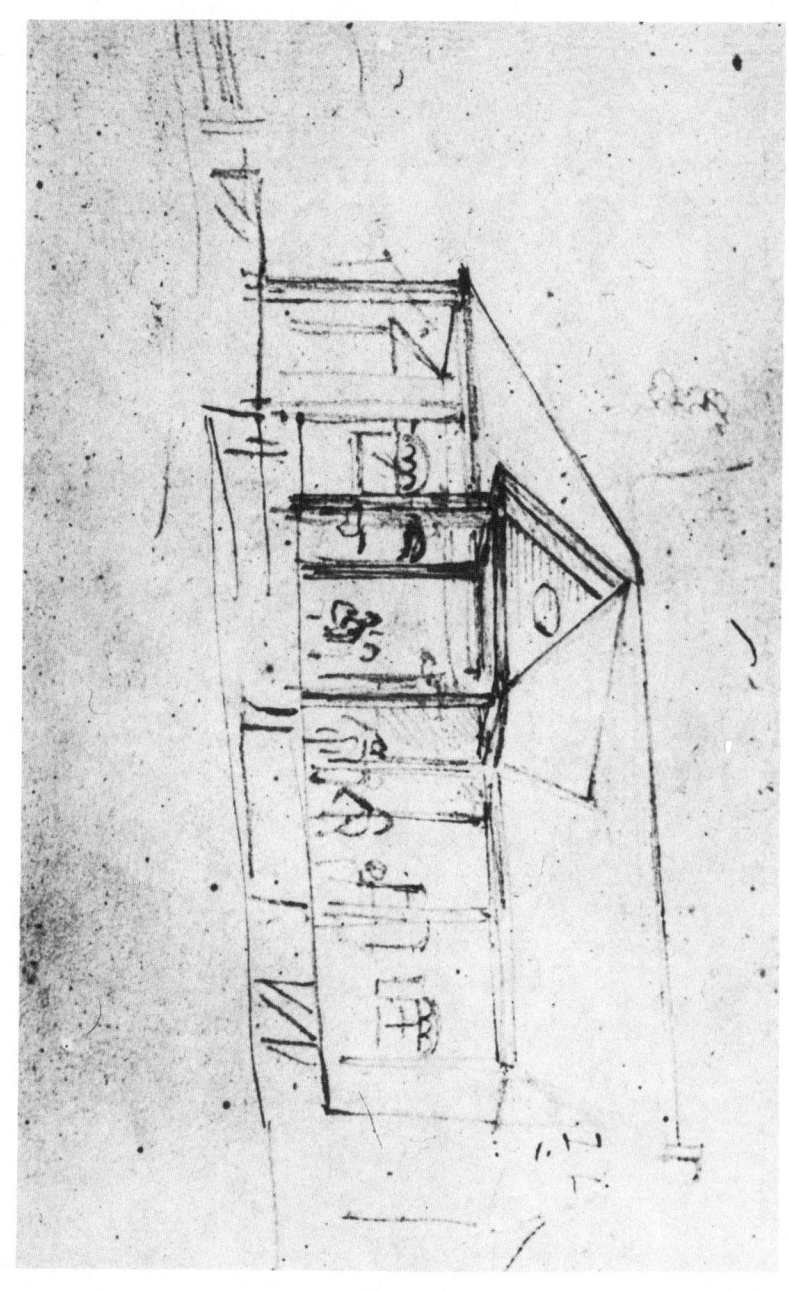

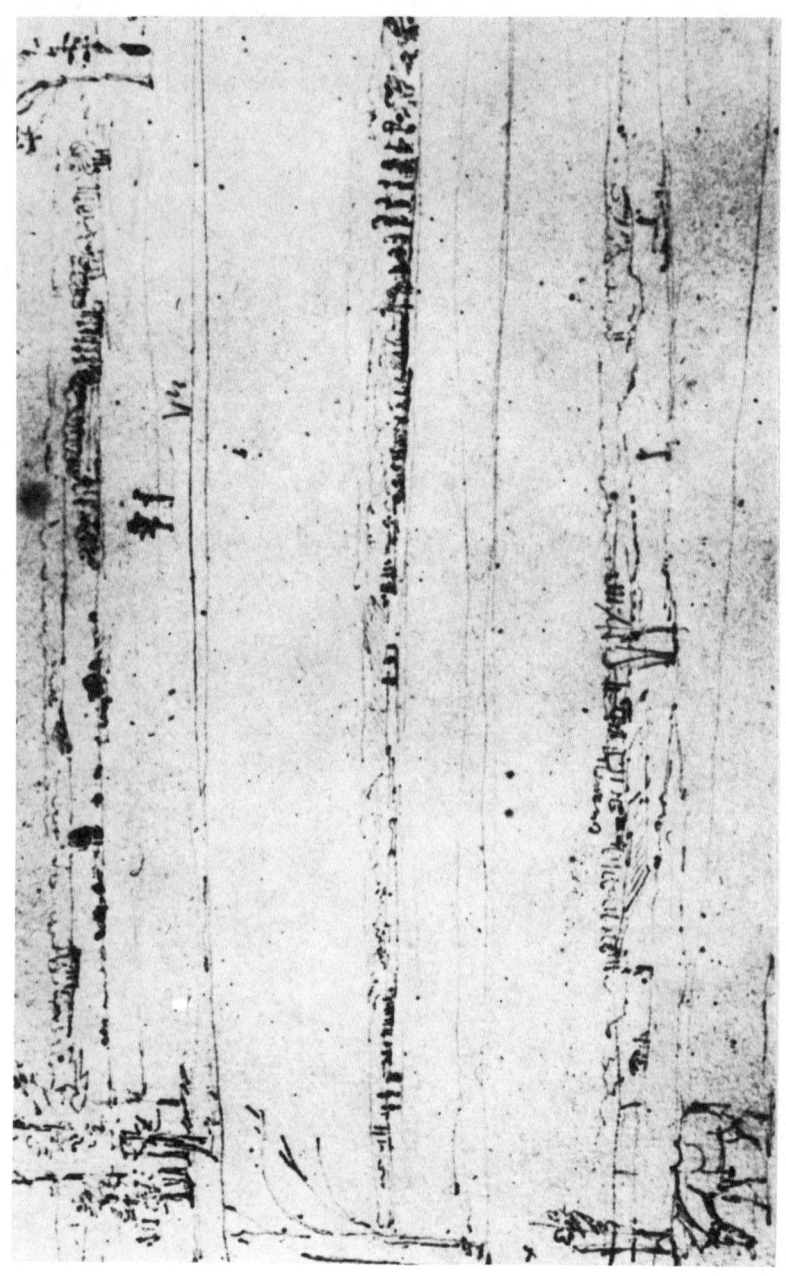

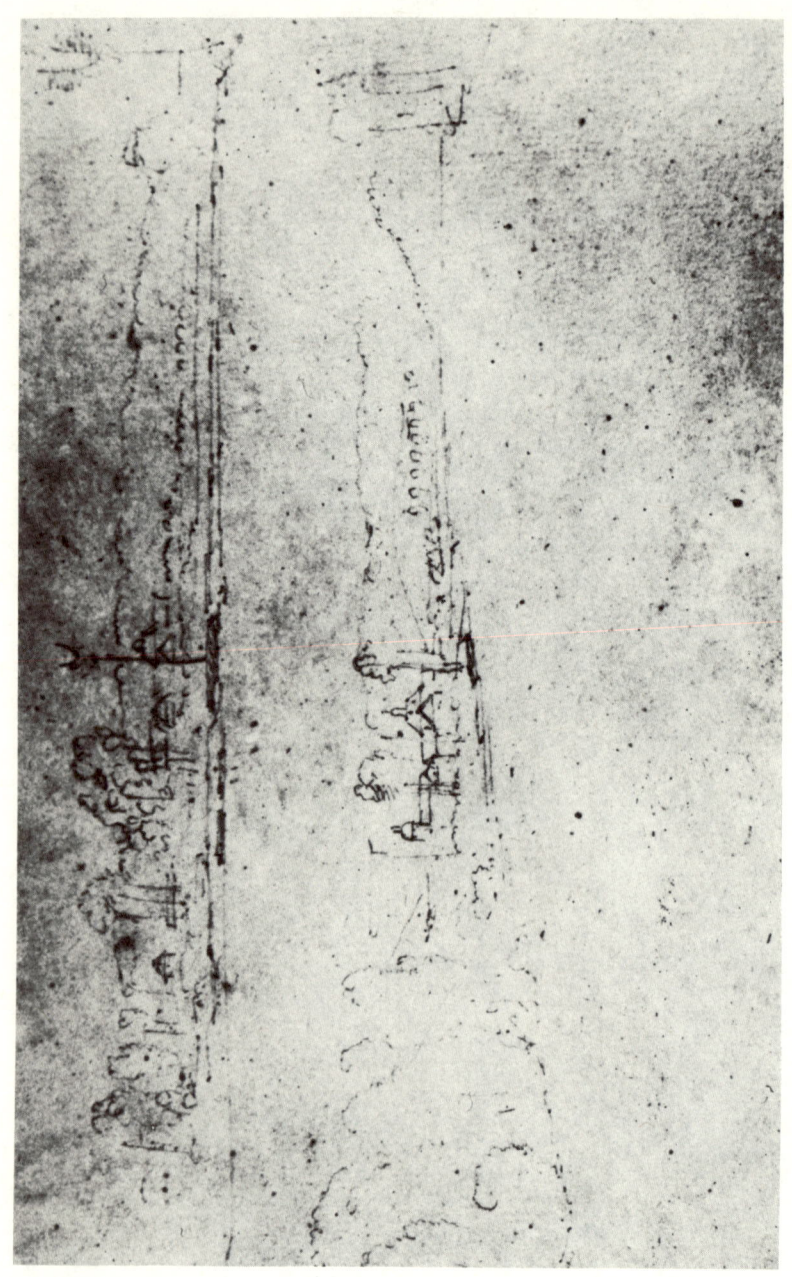

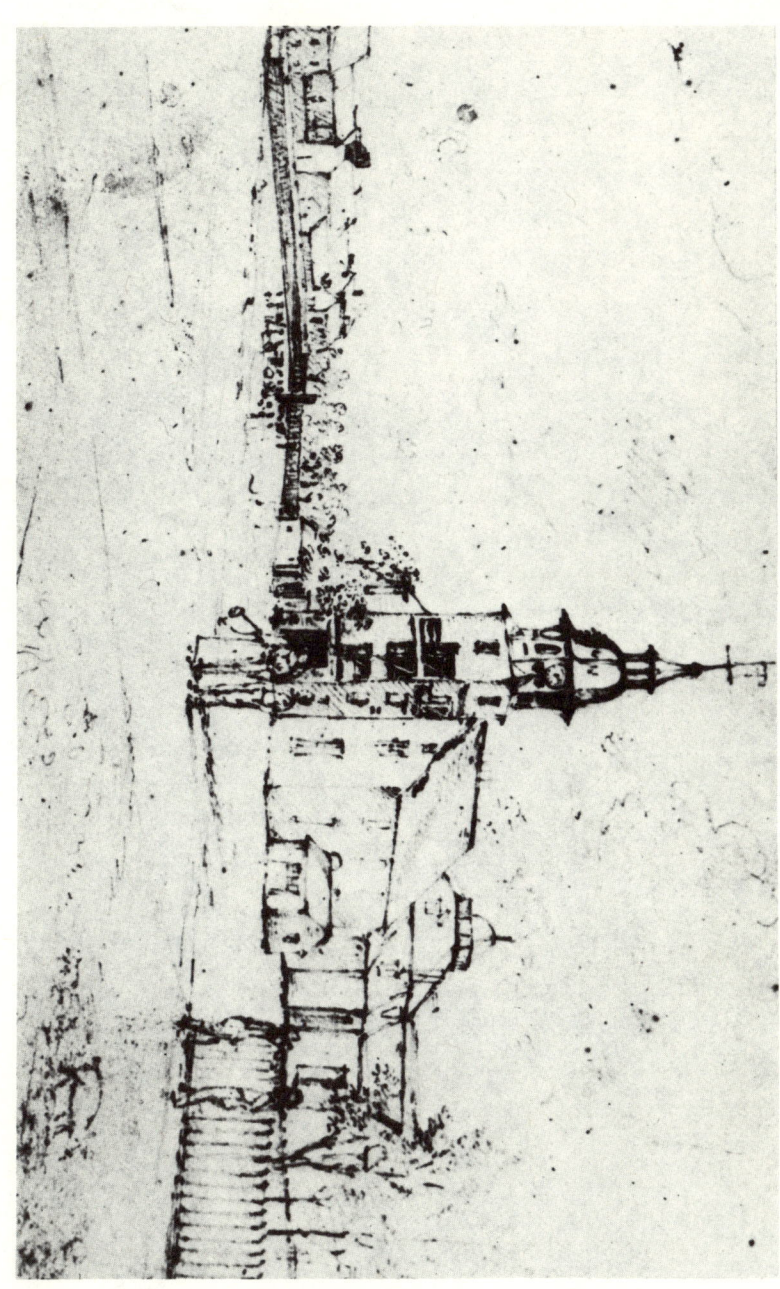

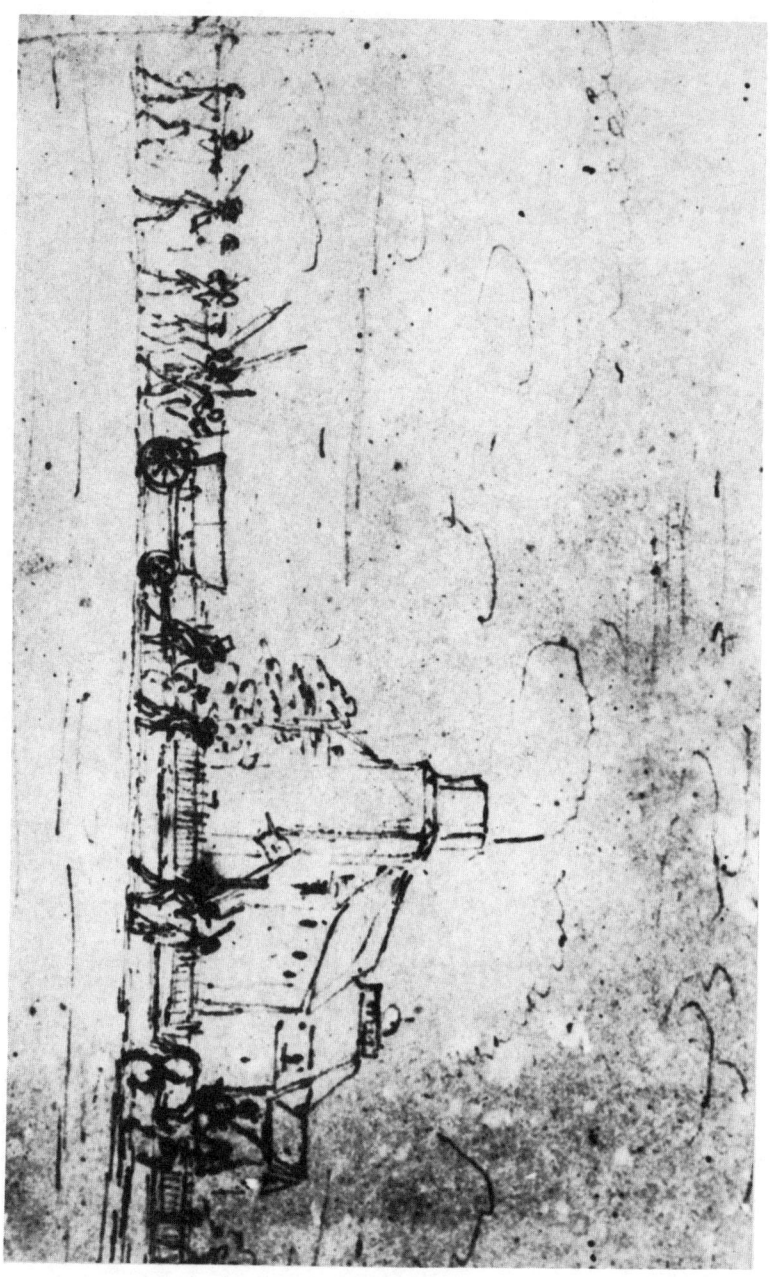

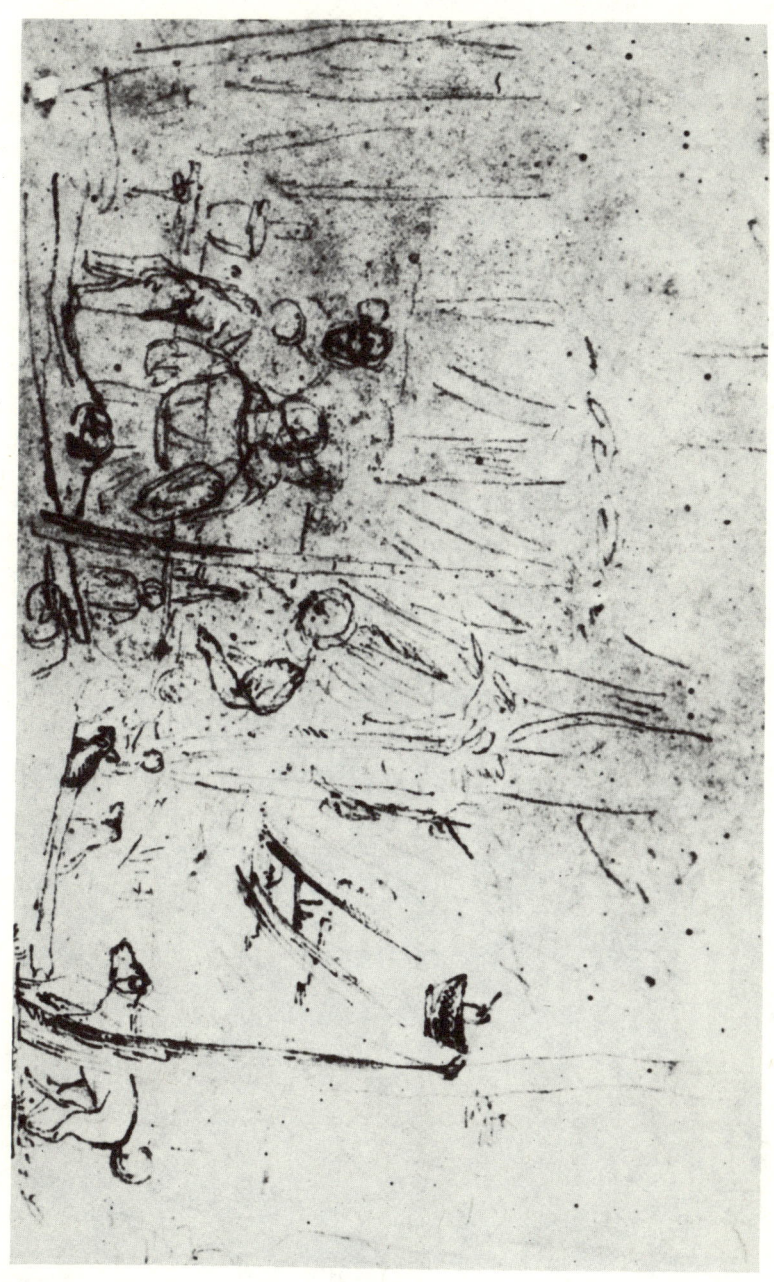

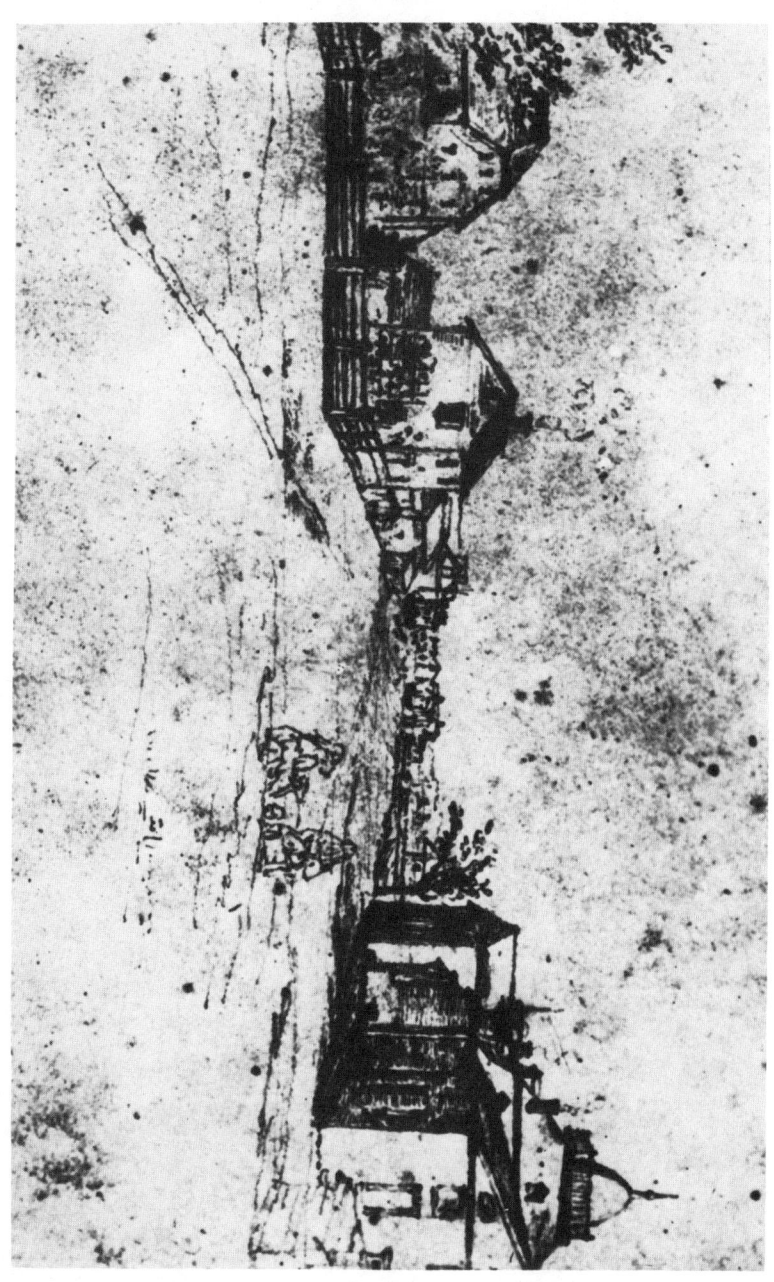

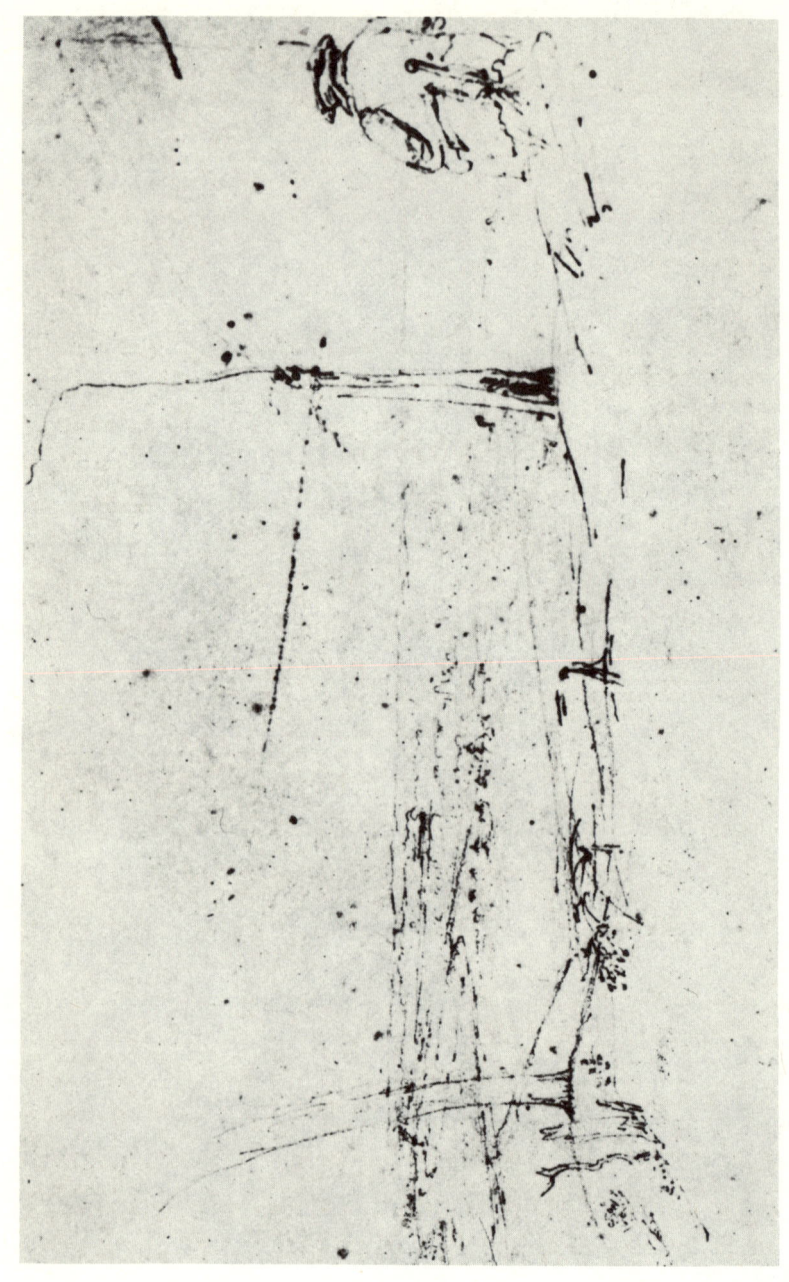

751

753

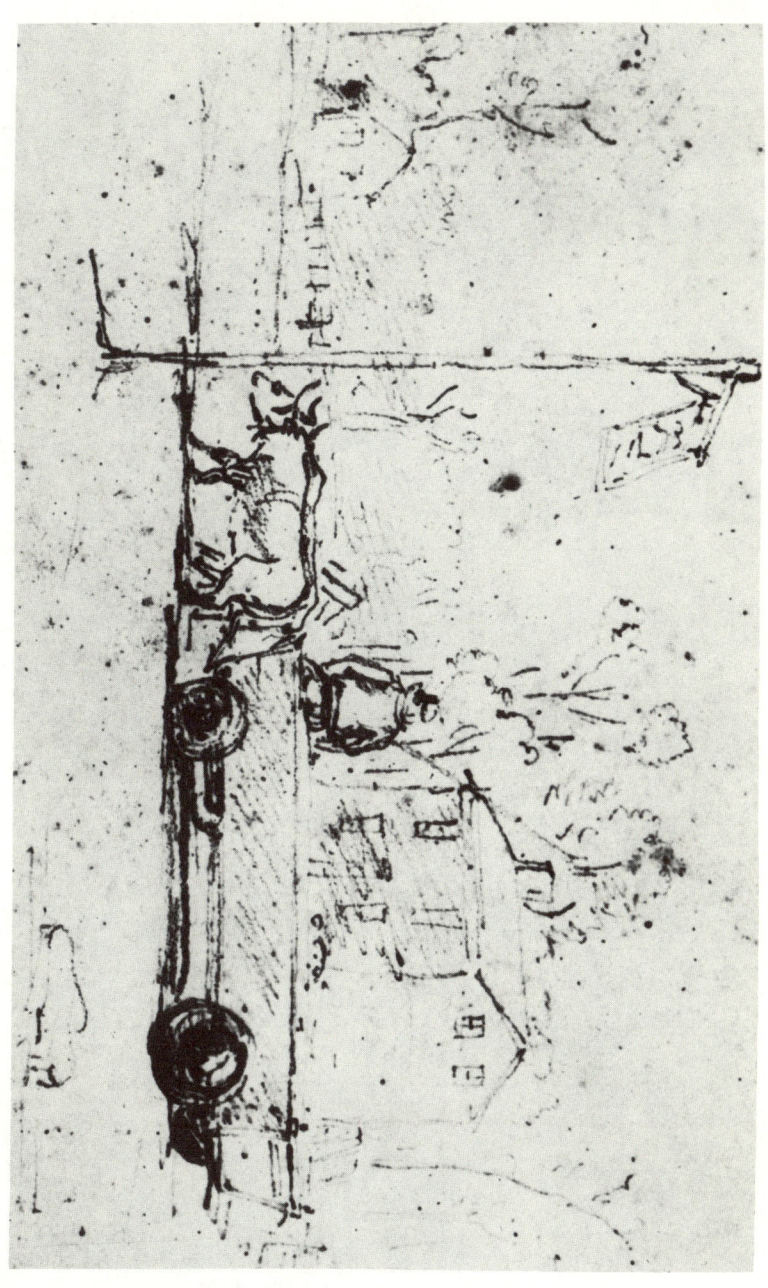